ILLUSTRATION ADAPTED FROM PHOTOGRAPHS OF CONNECTICUT HILL BY R. B. FISCHER

VOICES
from Connecticut Hill

VOICES
from Connecticut Hill

Recollections of Cornell Wildlife Students, 1930–1942

Harlan B. Brumsted, Mary Margaret Fischer, Richard B. Fischer, and Bradley L. Griffin

College of Agriculture and Life Sciences ◆ Cornell University ◆ Ithaca, New York

With a Foreword by Gustav A. Swanson and Robert A. McCabe

College of Agriculture and Life Sciences,
Cornell University

Department of Natural Resources, College of
Agriculture and Life Sciences, Cornell University,
Fernow Hall, Ithaca, NY 14853-3001

Printed in the United States of America

Drawing on page 127 by Clayton B. Seagears;
all other drawings by Fred Everett (reprinted, by
permission, from Bump, Darrow, Edminster, and
Crissey, *The Ruffed Grouse: Life History, Propagation, and Management*)

Library of Congress Catalog Card Number:
94-72544

ISBN 0-9605314-7-5

Printed using soy-based inks on recycled
paper with a minimum of 10 percent post-
consumer wastepaper

To all the Hillers,

past, present, and future

Returning to Cornell in autumn 1937 to pursue a master's degree, Al Bromley kept a diary that described his return to Connecticut Hill.

and moderation, into the serenity of Shangri-La.

I came upon a ludicrous explanation for the migration of birds today. It was the conclusion of an old time naturalist who was sure, when all his observations failed to prove otherwise, that birds migrated to the moon. The trip, according to this observer, took just sixty days and became quite reasonable when one realized that the birds would require very little energy to flit through the rarefied atmosphere. As for sleep, once on their way the birds could simply close their eyes and swing along dreaming no doubt of fat, juicy moon-worms. The moon must be full when they started and would be full again in 60 days to receive them.

OCT 3 NOTHING TO SAY.

OCT 4 I am surprised tonight not to find myself exhausted after tramping over Conn. Hill for the first Sunday of this year's survey. Perhaps the beauty of the day and the new fall clothing of the hill. Next Sunday the colors will be even finer but one couldn't ask for a more lovely contrast of reds, yellows and greens than we found in the clear sunshine of this perfect autumn day. A remarkable incident of the day was the discovery of two "drumming logs" which had been used very recently. One log had over 30 fresh grouse droppings, while the other had about 25. I don't know whether the records for drumming logs would show this to be unique or not. We also saw a junco carrying wisps of dry grass in its bill — purpose?. The brushy edges of the woods were fairly alive with robins feeding on choke-cherries and thorn apples.

I AM SURPRISED tonight not to find myself

exhausted after tramping over Connecticut Hill

for the first Sunday of this year's survey.

Perhaps it was the beauty of the

day and the new fall clothing of the

hill. Next Sunday the color

will be even finer, but one couldn't

ask for a more lovely contrast of reds,

yellows, and greens than we found in the

clear sunshine of this perfect autumn day.

A remarkable incident of the day was the

discovery of two drumming logs which

had been used very recently.

Albert W. Bromley ◆ October 4, 1937

CONTENTS

Contents

ix

Pioneering a New Profession

THE NEW YORK STATE ruffed grouse investigation is unique in the history of American wildlife conservation. Wildlife management became a recognized profession with the formation of the Wildlife Society in 1936 and 1937, but there had been several years of related activity, including prominently this New York project. Among its notable features was the appropriation by the New York State Legislature of $10,000 to initiate the research and the close cooperation displayed among sportsmen, the legislature, and the executive branch of the state government. Consider also the thoroughness and length of the investigation, from 1930 to 1942, and of its final report, a 915-page, six-pound tome that is still the most comprehensive publication on the biology and management of this revered American game bird.

This remarkable volume, *Voices from Connecticut Hill: Recollections of Cornell Wildlife Students, 1930–1942*, memorializes the young men, including many Cornell University students, who participated in the field research. After graduation a high proportion of them continued in wildlife work as a lifetime career, and many joined the Wildlife Society, some as charter members. The first leader of the investigation, Gardiner Bump, also served the new Wildlife Society as chairman of the committee that developed its constitution and bylaws.

The leading wildlife organization at the time the grouse project was initiated was the American Game Protective Association, which, starting in 1915, sponsored an annual conference on American game. The conferences were primarily devoted to game protection and game farming until the late 1920s, when Aldo Leopold and Cornell professor Arthur A. Allen began to attend and report on their research. Allen's early studies of ruffed grouse inspired the beginning of the New York State project and helped influence the formation of the Wildlife Society. He became the second president, succeeding Rudolf Bennitt of Missouri.

Aldo Leopold's leadership as the father of American wildlife management is unquestioned, resting on writing *An American Game Policy* (1930), *Report on a Game Survey of the North*

Central States (1931), and his classic textbook, *Game Management* (1933), and the professorship he held in wildlife management at the University of Wisconsin, established in 1933 and supported by the Wisconsin Alumni Research Foundation. Those accomplishments do not overshadow, however, the importance of developments in New York State and at Cornell University in establishing the profession and the Wildlife Society as nationwide in scope.

The ruffed grouse project resulted in the formation of the Bureau of Game as a permanent wildlife-management unit and in the creation of the Wildlife Research Center at Delmar, New York, which has an enviable record of outstanding wildlife studies.

Though the New York State ruffed grouse investigation began more than sixty years ago, many of the participants still keep in touch with each other at meetings or in correspondence. They recall the camaraderie they felt and share their pride in having participated. It is gratifying that their contribution is being commemorated in this manner. It recognizes the pioneer role that New York State and Cornell University played in North American wildlife conservation.

Gustav A. Swanson

A Salute to the Hewers and Carriers

THIS HEART-WARMING record of those who labored in the "trenches" on Connecticut Hill reflects the soul and spirit of the multifaceted project that became the classic reference on ruffed grouse. This fascinating book would not have had the same import or impact if it had been written at the same time and as a companion volume to *The Ruffed Grouse*.

Time distilled the essence of the Connecticut Hill experience and delivers it here in the words of those who toiled there. Most were Cornell University students, the "Hillers" of this story. Youthful and regardless of social or economic background, they became field-wise and woods-smart on Connecticut Hill, and in these pages some proudly display their scars of battle in recalling the lessons learned.

The often mundane slogging through the pleasure and pain of changing seasons and workload was enlivened by pranks that co-workers and nature played on the new and unsuspecting. The accounts are lucidly and unabashedly told by those who were party to the fun side of fieldwork. Not all Hillers were hellers, however.

Almost all vividly remember the scenic beauty of their workplace in sound, sight, and even taste (of the water). Perhaps these accounts lend credence to the obvious dictum that wildlife professionals must accept part of their salary in scenery.

The Hillers who became professional wildlife biologists were eminently successful. As important perhaps is that the nonbiologists obtained a rapport with the out-of-doors that enriched their lives in whatever endeavor they undertook. The rigorous discipline of gathering precise field data on Connecticut Hill could not fail to underpin any work ethic in any job or profession.

The Great Depression was everywhere present in financial need, frugality, privation, resolve, and striving. This narrative describes one example where college students had to work their way to a diploma. Twenty-cent-an-hour jobs, seven-dollar-a-week room and board, and a peanut-butter-and-jelly world moved the Hillers to commencement day. As one Hiller put it, the problem "was money—no one had any." How would one duplicate the indomitable spirit that was the driving force of the work ethic on Connecticut Hill without giving today's students, one and all, a touch of depression poverty?

No long-term study in wildlife management can escape or deny the human element that is implicit in the mechanics of a field effort by dedicated people. The Hillers were young men in need of a job but motivated by the contribution they were making to the understanding of America's premier upland game bird. In the outdoor laboratory that was Connecticut Hill, an indelible learning experience took place for that special group of men, who here share their thoughts and remembrances of a

heady time long gone. They fit Aldo Leopold's observation on teaching: "The object is to teach the student to see the land, to understand what he sees, and enjoy what he understands." The Hillers saw, understood, and enjoyed.

Esprit de corps, friendship, teamwork, and superb leadership were hallmarks that surfaced in these recollections of the fun, pathos, camaraderie, and learning that survived the years, to be relived in anecdotes of days in the sun (also rain, wind, cold, and snow).

The authors of *The Ruffed Grouse* credited those who had gathered and compiled the basic data as "the real hewers of wood and carriers of water." In the end, although their presence and efforts are hidden in tables and graphs, the Cornell Hillers may take a belated bow on behalf of all who labor to understand and conserve our wildlife heritage.

Robert A. McCabe

WHILE THE FRUITS of their labors constitute a classic volume in the annals of North American wildlife research, this is the first published account of the lives and times of the young men who gathered field data in New York State's renowned thirteen-year ruffed grouse investigation, initiated in 1930.

This volume commemorates all who participated in those pioneering studies at field sites across the state. The human dimensions of the grouse investigation are of special interest because of the pervasive influences of those times. The investigation was bracketed by the Great Depression and World War II and spanned a notably dynamic and expansive period in the development of policy and programs of natural resource conservation, particularly of wildlife and soil conservation.

In these pages we introduce the Hillers, those who did fieldwork for the investigation on Connecticut Hill, near Ithaca. Most of them were Cornell undergraduates. Four of them demonstrated special strengths in the research, became survey leaders, and ultimately wrote its monumental final report. The human aspects of the investigation also have a leader, whose enthusiasm for the survey experience and love of the Hill are unmatched. He is Benjamin O. Bradley, a native of Spencer, New York, and a 1934 graduate of Cornell University. Ben majored in agricultural economics, was on the Hill during four successive years, 1931 through 1934, and earned varsity letters in baseball for two seasons' play.

During my first full-time professional role in wildlife (1949–51), I worked on Pittman-Robertson project 48-D, the development of wildlife habitat on farmlands in western New York. Ben was my program supervisor. He sparked some impressive accomplishments, and his inspection tours were an inspiration and a delight. However, after 1951 we rarely saw each other. With his retirement in 1971 and his move to California, Ben became a distant memory, until 1982, when he presided at the opening banquet during a Hiller reunion in Ithaca. He integrated reminiscences with short speeches and set the stage for remarks by Dr. Gardiner Bump, the first leader of the investigation, who was present with his wife, Johnnie. Ben was clearly a contemporary leader among these Hiller alumni.

I next heard from him in early 1986, when he wrote to Ray Oglesby, then chairman of the Department of Natural Resources at Cornell, to enlist participation of the department along with the New York State Department of Environmental Conservation to perpetuate the best interests of Connecticut Hill. Ben furnished copies of his correspondence to three of his "stalwarts," as he called us: Don Spittler '41, Brad Griffin '61, and me, Ph.D. '54—all friends from his postwar wildlife-management days. He made several suggestions and asked us to select a way to promote interest in the Hill and in its historic importance to wildlife conservation.

Meeting in June 1986, we recommended that the Connecticut Hill Student Internship Fund be established as an endowment to support paid undergraduate internships in field studies. Ben was delighted, and once we obtained approval from the College of Agriculture and Life Sciences at Cornell, he pledged a major sum to the cause. He also helped us organize a steering committee and finalize plans for fund raising. As news of the internship spread, it was received enthusiastically.

At the next Hiller reunion at Cornell, in June 1988, Ben urged us to gather material on the lighter side of the survey. "What a story it would be!" he exclaimed. I don't recall whether Ben looked in my direction when he extended the challenge, but I resolved to pursue the opportunity when time allowed. It would be a chance to thank these men for their hard work and generosity in making the internship fund a success. But how to do it? What would be a workable approach? Whom could I get to help me?

I checked in with a friend of Ben's and mine who had helped set up the internship fund—fellow stalwart Brad Griffin, supervisor of natural resources in our regional Department of Environmental Conservation office. He was interested, and several months later, when he retired from his post, he would be able to include the Hiller project among his retirement activities. Who else? I thought of a couple with whom I had once worked a great deal: Richard B. Fischer, professor emeritus of environmental education, and Mary Margaret Fischer, experienced writer and editor. They too were interested.

In May 1991 our Hiller writing project budded with the spring flora. We defined our objectives for a commemorative publication and constituted ourselves as a team of editors to pursue it. We developed a packet to use in soliciting written reminiscences from the Hillers covering their student days and mailed it in November. Return packets soon appeared and kept coming in throughout the winter. The quality of the contributions was superb. Thirty-seven Hillers responded to the initial request, a return rate of 76 percent, and another, not on our original list, sent reminiscences later. We editors organized the anecdotes into sections and prepared introductions for them. Our editing was light, as we endeavored to preserve individual writing styles.

In this volume we present the human dimension of New York's unique ruffed grouse investigation, told by the Hillers themselves and illustrated with photos they have treasured for more than a half-century. We are proud to honor those men for their pioneering accomplishments in wildlife research and to express our gratitude to them for initiating the internship fund, which will provide the financial means for today's students to have learning opportunities like those they had experienced on Connecticut Hill.

Ben Bradley predicted a great story. We believe he and his colleagues have written it!

Harlan B. Brumsted

ACKNOWLEDGMENTS

IN THE DEPARTMENT of Natural Resources at Cornell, site of all preparation and processing of project communications and manuscripts, there are many to thank: Elizabeth Dempsey-Loid, administrative manager; Nancy L. Bowers, word-processing specialist; Deborah W. Grover, Lisa Bishop-Oltz, Mary E. Mills, Ellen C. Harris, and Linda A. Lattin, administrative assistants; Joan Bartlett-Peck and Tamara M. Shollenberger, accounts representatives; and work-study students Jason Petyk and Kevin J. Schroder.

Lisa A. Maloney, natural resources major and 1992 graduate, our first Connecticut Hill intern, helped us establish document files of Hiller essays, performed library research, and facilitated our progress in many ways.

Others whose assistance we gratefully acknowledge are Cornell vice president Henrik Dullea, professor emeritus of natural resources Oliver H. Hewitt, and natural resources faculty members Aaron N. Moen, John W. Kelley, and Charles R. Smith.

Herbert E. Doig, assistant commissioner, and Marc S. Gerstman, general counsel and deputy commissioner, New York State Department of Environmental Conservation, granted permission to quote from *The Ruffed Grouse* and to use the delightful sketches by Fred Everett and Clayton Seagears.

Graphic designer Phil Wilson and copy editor Lynn Colvin were ideal consultants, brimming with ideas and expertise and stimulating us to do our best work.

Seven people who had no direct connection with the Hillers agreed to review our manuscript. For their generous, expert assistance we are especially grateful to William G. Boldt, assistant dean for public affairs and development, College of Agriculture and Life Sciences, Cornell; Daniel J. Decker, chairman and associate professor, Department of Natural Resources, Cornell; John A. Gustafson, retired chairman and professor, Department of Biological Sciences, State University of New York College at Cortland; Laurence R. Jahn, immediate past president, Wildlife Management

Institute; Judith Lutes, teacher and librarian; William MacLeish, essayist, author, and editor; and Patricia McClary, associate counsel, Cornell. Their criticisms and suggestions were of enormous benefit.

Two distinguished senior academicians in the wildlife field also furnished outstanding contributions: Gustav A. Swanson and Robert A. McCabe, who both contributed to the foreword. Professor Swanson was the first head of Cornell's Department of Conservation, 1948–66 (the department later became the Department of Natural Resources). Professor McCabe succeeded Aldo Leopold as chairman of the Department of Wildlife Ecology at the University of Wisconsin–Madison, 1948–75.

To have had the full support of Professors Ray T. Oglesby, James P. Lassoie, and Daniel J. Decker, the men who chaired the Department of Natural Resources during the recent years of Hiller activities, has been truly gratifying.

David L. Call, dean of Cornell's College of Agriculture and Life Sciences, identified the Hiller story as important college history that deserved publication and approved initial funding of the first printing of this book. His continuing support has heartened us immeasurably.

We are indebted to the many Hillers who shared their photographic treasures with us, and we particularly thank Robert W. Darrow and George B. Elliott for their perseverance in our quest for the negatives of their high-quality photographs. We also appreciate the help of Mary Morris Kelsey and Evelyn Steinman Cook in lending both prints and negatives from their late husbands' files.

For their prompt and generous responses to our inquiries about photographs, we recognize David G. Allen and Prof. Kraig Adler. Also making loans in response to specific inquiries were Angie Berchielli, Edward Makowski, and Wayne Trimm. Nancy L. Dean, collections assistant for the Division of Rare and Manuscript Collections in the Carl A. Kroch Library at Cornell, helped with several difficult searches, as did John Sterling, development officer in the College of Agriculture and Life Sciences; David P. Wohlhueter, Cornell's director of sports information; and Laura Lynch-Benjamin, administrative coordinator in University Photography.

We thank Donald S. Erdman for lending us four of his diaries to photograph, and we thank Albert W. Bromley's widow, Alice, and son, Peter, for lending Al's diary.

We greatly appreciate the encouragement and unceasing assistance provided by Evelyn Brumsted. Her help was invaluable to us.

Among our Hiller contributing authors eight have played a special role. They are the committee formed in 1986 to steer development of the Connecticut Hill Student Internship Fund. Remaining active as close advisors and assistants throughout the past three years, they critically reviewed two versions of the manuscript and were often called on to respond to our needs for specialized knowledge and sage advice. With much respect, and deep and abiding appreciation, we name our special advisors and supporters in this enterprise: Benjamin O. Bradley, Walter F. Crissey, Robert W. Darrow, Albert G. Hall, W. Mason Lawrence, Richard E. Reynolds, C. William Severinghaus, and Donald J. Spittler.

To those committeemen, and to all the Hiller contributing authors, we express gratitude not only for the inspiration of their words and deeds in behalf of this project, but for their abundant good humor, which we found to be contagious.

Yes, since spring 1991, we editors have enjoyed many good times together, often in the company of Lynn, Phil, and Evelyn. Our sincere thanks to all involved in this endeavor for helping make the process as memorable as the outcome!

I N 1947 THE NEW YORK STATE Conservation Department published *The Ruffed Grouse: Life History, Propagation, Management.* It is a beautifully crafted tome summarizing thirteen years of field observation and data collection. It not only documents a pioneering scientific study of the grouse but remains the classic, definitive study of this magnificent bird.

While many labored on the study and its publication, the listed authors are Gardiner Bump, Robert W. Darrow, Frank C. Edminster, and Walter F. Crissey. The senior author, Gardiner Bump, wrote the preface in May 1942. His first two sentences provide the foundation for this introduction: "In a scientific report such as this, there is little room for personalities or individual feelings. Only in the preface can one give expression to thoughts quite unscientific but undeniably human."

Thus the door is opened now for *Voices from Connecticut Hill: Recollections of Cornell Wildlife Students, 1930–1942,* which is not a scientific report but rather focuses on the people who were involved and the times in which they lived. It is mostly told by the participants themselves in recollections, anecdotes, and diary entries.

In the narrowest view, it tells the background of this study of the ruffed grouse. Much of the fieldwork was carried out on Connecticut Hill, now a state wildlife-management area of more than ten thousand acres in Tompkins and Schuyler Counties in central New York.

Cornell University played a major role in the historic study. Prof. Arthur A. Allen laid the groundwork for the direction of this early wildlife research and selected the study area. The New York State Conservation Department, which sponsored the pioneer investigation, valued Dr. Allen's advice in this inquiry and at other times. From the beginning he was its scientific advisor. Other Cornell professors lent support to the study as it proceeded. Cornell students, mostly College of Agriculture undergraduates, constituted the fieldwork force that carried out much of the study.

Significantly, Cornell and its professors provided an environment that nourished this new field of inquiry and led to the development of professional education for natural resource researchers and managers.

But in a larger sense, this is a story of America and Americans in the 1930s and early 1940s. It provides historical insight into an important period in the continuing evolution of our philosophy of natural resource conservation. And through the anecdotal vignettes we are given the profiles of people who strove to improve their lot during the Great Depression, then faced the harsh realities of World War II, and returned to their stewardship as leaders, exhibiting good humor and a positive outlook.

To give a dimension of historical chronology to the grouse study, we note that by the early 1900s sportsmen in New York had recognized that grouse populations were cyclic. In 1907 a population survey was undertaken by the sole method of sending postcard questionnaires to hunters and game protectors. After a subsequent population low during World War I, the state Conservation Commission made its initial turn for advice to Dr. Allen. He was, by then, Cornell's first professor in ornithology, widely respected as a gentleman and a scholar.

In 1928 low populations again stimulated sportsmen's concern. The Conservation Depart-

ment closed the season for that year and called a conference in August 1929. Heeding Dr. Allen's advice, the department moved to fund and inaugurate the grouse investigation.

In October 1929 the stock market crashed. That event coincided with the acceleration of Dust Bowl conditions in the Middle West. Crops failed, farmland literally blew away, and farmers took to the road like refugees. The prairie wetlands that supported waterfowl nesting dried up, and so did waterfowl populations.

Hilltop farms in the East, like those that then existed on Connecticut Hill, had been cropped to a state of depletion. The families who lived on the tracts were hard put to subsist.

The Great Depression had arrived across the land, with dimensions of adversity in economics, social structure, and natural resources.

In 1910 Franklin Delano Roosevelt had chaired the Fish and Game Committee of the New York State Senate. Later he served as governor of New York. He was elected to the presidency in 1932 and took office in March 1933. Soon a host of new national programs affected the events of the grouse study and Connecticut Hill.

Purchases of game refuge lands on the Hill began in 1929 with money from New York's new Conservation Fund, a repository for proceeds from the sale of hunting and fishing licenses. In the early 1930s acquisition efforts were substantially accelerated by "farm relief" programs of

the new administration. Assistance to destitute families was the immediate target of agencies such as the federal Emergency Relief Administration (1934). Then, in 1935, that effort and several related ones were combined into the federal Resettlement Administration, which focused both on getting families off unproductive lands and on treating urgent resource-conservation needs such as erosion control. In New York State the work of reforestation and game habitat improvement were highlighted immediately. Today Connecticut Hill is the largest of New York's wildlife-management areas, as the former game refuges are now known.

The Civilian Conservation Corps was formed in 1933, and the Hill was one of the public land areas where unemployed young men conducted forestry and wildlife conservation work, as well as improvements to roads and bridges.

The National Youth Administration provided an additional source of wages to the student fieldworkers. The grouse study offered outdoor work on Saturdays and Sundays with low but sure wages for those willing, whether or not they owned suitable footwear and clothing.

In December 1941 America was plunged into World War II. The last of the fieldwork for the study was completed in 1942. As one of the smaller consequences of the war, publication of *The Ruffed Grouse* was delayed until 1947.

A Call to Stewardship

President Franklin D. Roosevelt's interest in developing a working conservation ethic, and his commitment to do so, is evident in this February 3, 1936, greeting to the first North American Wildlife Conference. It was a call to stewardship and a renaissance of spirit.

I regret my inability to extend a personal welcome to you or to participate personally in your discussion. Because this is impossible, I have asked Secretary Wallace to convey my best wishes for a most successful and profitable meeting.

It has long been my feeling that there has been lack of a full and complete public realization of our wildlife plight, of the urgency of it, and of the many social and economic values that wildlife has to our people. This, and my firm belief in the ability of the American people to face facts, to analyze problems, and to work out a program which might remedy the situation, is what impelled me to call the North American Wildlife Conference.

Our present wildlife situation is more than a local one. It is national and international. I sincerely hope that with the help of good neighbors to the north and south of us, your conference will unite upon a common purpose and a common program.

You have been told that this conference is an open forum; that it is entirely autonomous; that its future is subject to its own decisions. This is as it should be, for it makes it possible for you as representatives of thousands of wildlife organizations with millions of interested and zealous members to make effective progress in restoring and conserving the vanishing wildlife resources of a continent.

Sincerely,
Franklin D. Roosevelt

◆ *This poster, used to publicize the first North American Wildlife Conference, was reprinted by the Wildlife Management Institute for the conference's fiftieth anniversary (original art by Lynn Bogue Hunt, 1878–1960).*

A decade after the publication of *The Ruffed Grouse,* I became an employee of the New York State Conservation Department. Consequently I worked with many of the Hillers and met a substantial number who were employed elsewhere. Without exception, I enjoyed knowing them and learning from them. I was privileged to join them in our work and at play. And now my fellow editors and I are privileged to introduce them in the following pages. In sharing their experiences, we hope that the spirit of mentoring that underlies the making and the telling of these stories will be continued by future generations.

Bradley L. Griffin

THIS BOOK *is not only for the Hillers but by the Hillers. The contributing authors are listed below. After the name of each Hiller is the place he was living when he entered Cornell or another university. At the end of the entry is his current residence. Please note that although Tom Baskous was the only Hiller named here who joined the New York State Department of Environmental Conservation in 1970, the year it was formed, all those who were working for the Conservation Department at that time became DEC employees.*

Thirty-eight Hillers contributed the reminiscences that constitute a substantial portion of this volume. We thank them for their generous, thoughtful, and well-written responses.

Athan A. (Tom) Baskous, Schenectady, NY. An environmental engineer with the New York State Department of Health, Tom joined the Department of Environmental Conservation in a department merger in 1970 and was appointed its regional director in the Albany area. Schenectady.

Dirck Benson, Ukiah, CA. A Cornell master's program launched Dirck's New York State Conservation Department career in pheasant and waterfowl research—a career capped by his position as supervisor of fish and wildlife in the eastern Adirondacks. Saranac Lake, NY.

Benjamin O. Bradley, Spencer, NY. Emissary for New York State's superintendent of game during the thirties, Ben became a game manager in the central New York counties and statewide leader of habitat restoration on private lands. He retired in 1971. Pasadena, CA.

Royce B. Brower, Morrisville, NY. Royce's thirty years with the U.S. Department of Agriculture's Soil Conservation Service was mostly spent working in the central New York area where he had grown up—Madison and Otsego Counties. West Eaton, NY, and Arcadia, FL.

Greenleaf T. Chase, Newburyport, MA. An honored authority on wilderness wildlife, notably raptors, Greenie had a New York State Conservation Department career in wildlife biology and management centered in the Adirondacks' high-peaks area. Saranac Lake, NY.

Paul W. Christner, Pavilion, NY. After receiving his B.S. degree in agriculture in 1938, Paul worked briefly for the U.S. Department of Agriculture near Oswego before returning home to make farming in Genesee County his career. Pavilion.

Ralph B. Colson, Schenectady, NY. Ralph worked as a wildlife biologist, based in the Division of Fish and Wildlife in Albany, where his administrative roles included coordinating land acquisition and serving as wildlife bureau chief. Schenectady.

Walter F. Crissey, Ithaca, NY. Walt's career with the U.S. Fish and Wildlife Service in research on, and management of, North American waterfowl was recognized with a Distinguished Service Medal from the U.S. Department of the Interior. Punta Gorda, FL.

Robert W. Darrow, Ashville, NY. Bob had a career in wildlife research, with the New York State Conservation Department, that was of exceptionally long duration and high productivity—fifty-eight years in all, nearly thirty-five as editor of the *New York Fish and Game Journal.* Delmar, NY.

Joseph Dell, Ithaca, NY. Joe's career in wildlife biology with New York State included long-term research on the cottontail rabbit, the administration of research, and the administration of the Division of Fish and Wildlife's environmental protection unit. Delmar, NY.

Nick Drahos, Lawrence, NY. Nick used his broad background and his talents in photography, writing, and teaching to foster growth and excellence in New York's postwar conservation education program. For six years he also headed Guam's wildlife research. Aurora, NY.

George B. Elliott, Fairport, NY. Commencing as a game biologist in central New York, George became wildlife manager in the Catskill region and then headed the New York State Department of Environmental Conservation's regulatory affairs unit in the Albany area. Cortland, NY.

Donald S. Erdman, New York City. Don's first position was scientific aide in the Division of Fishes, U.S. National Museum of Natural History; his principal career was as a fishery biologist to the government of Puerto Rico, from 1954 to 1984. Portland, OR.

Donald D. Foley, Watervliet, NY. As an avian biologist for the New York State Conservation Department, Don conducted research on waterfowl for many years and later supervised studies on bobwhite quail, ring-necked pheasant, and wild turkey. Delmar, NY.

Frederic D. Garrett, Ithaca, NY. Armed with a Ph.D. in zoology, Fred taught neuroanatomy at the University of Nebraska College of Medicine, Ohio State University, the University of Miami School of Medicine, and the University of British Columbia. Lacey, WA.

Eugene J. Gerberg, New York City. Gene is an honored adjunct professor at the University of Florida. He had an entomological consulting firm and a career in the army, including global missions for the World Health Organization and the Agency for International Development. Gainesville, FL.

John S. Grim, Delmar, NY. Initially an aquatic biologist with the New York State Conservation Department, John developed a commercial enterprise; he raises warm-water fish for stocking and consults with pond and lake owners. Rhinebeck, NY.

Albert G. Hall, Troy, NY. A career professional in the New York State Conservation Department, Al was named game manager when the Catskill district formed and ultimately became director of the Division of Fish and Wildlife. Stamford, NY, and Lehigh Acres, FL.

Arthur S. Hawkins, Batavia, NY. Art joined the U.S. Fish and Wildlife Service at Minneapolis, becoming flyway representative for the Mississippi Flyway; he was that vast region's principal waterfowl biologist at decision-making councils. Hugo, MN.

Warren J. Hewes, Chautauqua, NY. Although his career was not in conservation—Warren headed the personnel division of the Atlantic Research Corporation—his esteem for wildlife classes and Hiller days never waned. Fairfax, VA, and North Port, FL.

Kermit Kruse, Ithaca, NY. A tip Frank Edminster gave in a lecture led Kermit to a career in the Soil Conservation Service; he served three New York State soil conservation districts: Allegany, Cattaraugus, and Wyoming. Silver Springs, NY, and Yuma, AZ.

Cornelius W. (Neal) Kuhn, Buffalo, NY. After World War II Neal faced a tough choice: dairy farming in western New York or working as a wildlife biologist with New York State; farming won, and Neal says he's had his own 230-acre "preserve" too. West Valley, NY.

Robert E. Laubengayer, Ithaca, NY. Always treasuring memories of his Hiller days on the summer crew in 1938, Bob devoted his career to carpentry and cabinetmaking. He succumbed to advanced diabetes on June 25, 1992, in Ithaca.

W. Mason Lawrence, Brooktondale, NY. Mason advanced rapidly in the New York State Conservation Department—regional biologist, bureau chief, director of fish and wildlife, deputy commissioner—and he says his career was "rewarding and enjoyable." Brooktondale.

Charles I. Mason, Brewerton, NY. Chuck's career as wildlife research biologist with the New York State Conservation Department included waterfowl and upland game bird projects; he cites most success with turkey restoration. Clarksville, NY.

James C. Otis, Lowville, NY. After a start in fishery biology in Vermont, Jim joined the Boston office of the U.S. Fish and Wildlife Service and be-

came northeast regional supervisor of fishery management services. Ann Arbor, MI, and St. Augustine, FL.

Ransom I. (Rip) Page, Bergen, NY. Rip's career was in retail household appliances in Spencerport, New York. He especially enjoyed outings near the Hi-Tor Wildlife Management Area, which he helped develop in the thirties. Rip passed away June 29, 1993, in Canandaigua, NY.

Arch C. Petty, Coreys, NY. As a fishery biologist, Arch's name was synonymous with fisheries management in central New York; he served as the Conservation Department's regional fisheries manager at the Norwich and Cortland offices. Virgil, NY, and Sun City Center, FL.

Richard E. Reynolds, Sherburne, NY. Dick was foreman of New York State's Ithaca Game Farm from 1937 to 1975, and in recognition of his exemplary service, the state named the facility the Richard E. Reynolds Game Farm in 1974. Ithaca, NY, and North Port, FL.

Lionel E. Ross, Warrensburg, NY. Although in college Lionel concentrated in fish culture and limnology, he chose a career as land surveyor with the New York State Conservation Department's Division of Lands and Forests. Warrensburg.

Donald Schierbaum, Scotia, NY. Don devoted over forty years to his career with New York State, doing research on cottontail rabbits, waterfowl, and Hungarian partridge and concluding as regional supervisor for fish and wildlife on Long Island. Altamont, NY.

Herbert W. Schrauer, New York City. While Herb's career has been in real estate, a continuing interest in wildlife has given his life an artistic turn: he creates animals out of driftwood. Malden-on-Hudson, NY, and Lake Como, FL.

C. William Severinghaus, Ithaca, NY. Bill's notably productive New York State career in white-tailed deer research and management brought honors from the entire wildlife profession and from alumni of his college at Cornell. Voorheesville, NY, and Umatilla, FL.

Donald J. Spittler, Lake View, NY. An honored public servant, Don had a career of twenty-seven years in wildlife management and land acquisition with New York State and fourteen years in appraisal with the federal office of Housing and Urban Development in Buffalo. Lake View.

Wayne Trimm, Syracuse, NY. Wayne, an environmental educator working mainly through writing and painting, is widely recognized for his illustrations in the *Conservationist* and many other magazines and books. Hoosick Falls, NY.

Adna H. (Sarge) Underhill, Summit, NJ. After thirteen years as New Jersey's director of fish and game, Sarge became assistant director of the U.S. Bureau of Outdoor Recreation—a role for which the U.S. Department of the Interior awarded him a citation for meritorious service. Tucson, AZ.

Harvey F. Warner, Van Etten, NY. Harvey started in land acquisition with the New York State Conservation Department and then joined the U.S. Fish and Wildlife Service, becoming realty officer for the entire thirteen-state northeast region. Van Etten.

Earl A. Westervelt, Ithaca, NY. After several positions in wildlife management and administration with the New York State Conservation Department, Westy became the Division of Conservation Education's senior editor and then its director. Albany, NY, and Fort Myers, FL.

These Hillers are quoted posthumously:

Albert W. Bromley, Waterport, NY. From broad experience in fishery and wildlife roles, Al became noted and honored for his leadership of the Division of Conservation Education, where he pioneered conservation education centers, regional educators, and cooperation in teacher education. As editor of the *Conservationist,* he led it to new heights of circulation and award-winning recognition. Al passed away at the age of seventy-six on November 1, 1987, in Fort Myers, FL.

Paul M. Kelsey, Ithaca, NY. After World War II Paul was New York State's district game manager in Ithaca, and then he branched out into conservation education in the central New York region. He became well known for his weekly column, "Conservation Comments," which regularly appeared in newspapers statewide. As field editor for the *Conservationist,* Paul was widely recognized for his range of contributions to the magazine. He died at age sixty-five on April 21, 1986, in Dryden, NY.

VOICES
from Connecticut Hill

A photograph of Cornell University, "far above Cayuga's waters," taken from Sage Hall by Ithaca photographer John P. Troy in the 1920s

CHAPTER ONE

Off to College

STARTING OUT ON A CORNELL CAREER

WHERE TO GO TO COLLEGE *was a pivotal decision for the future Hillers as the decade of the 1920s ended and the 1930s began. But when they filled out their applications, these young men had little inkling of just how pivotal. The furthest thing from their minds was that they were to be pioneers in the fast-emerging field of wildlife management. They and their families approached the college decision pragmatically.*

The depression had dashed many dreams of attending college in faraway places. Instead the crucial issue was how to pay for an education. A nearby college meant a low-cost education, and for many of these prospective students nearby meant Cornell. Besides, the College of Agriculture was tuition-free for New York State residents.

The economic reality of the times was not the only consideration. Some Hillers had family ties to Cornell, and others wanted to pursue their interest in the out-of-doors, in wildlife, and particularly in birds.

Art Hawkins's interest in birds, an interest that led him to Cornell and has lasted a lifetime, was encouraged by a customer on his paper route. Art was the lone member of his family who had that interest and who liked to hunt and fish:

Luckily my parents tolerated, and even supported, my strange cravings to spend every spare moment hunting, fishing, trapping, and camping. We lived within the city limits of Batavia, New York, but open fields and woods were only minutes away. We didn't own a car. A bicycle provided transportation when walking was impractical.

TONY DeCAMILLO

◆ *The pocket-size bird guides, by Chester A. Reed, introduced thousands to bird study in the early decades of this century. In the introductory pages the author urged bird protection. From 1910 to 1915 the guides cost $1.00 for a copy with a cloth cover and $1.25 for a leather-bound copy. Reed suggested getting one of each, for field and library use.*

My cruising radius was dictated by how far afield I could ramble and still be home in time to run my afternoon paper route.

A paper route required dedication and discipline, often tearing me away just as the fish started

biting, but it provided a small income and other rewards, such as interesting and valuable contacts. By strange co-incidence, the second customer along my route was named Brumsted. They had a son named Harlan, the same Harlan who will edit what I am now writing sixty years later.

Farther down Summit Street lived another customer, Fanny Bronson. She was the typical "little old lady in tennis shoes," the local authority on birds. When I stopped there to collect for the *Batavia Daily News,* she would talk about birds, gradually building my interest in them. She suggested that I get a copy of Reed's *Bird Guide* (I still have it) and, if possible, some field glasses. For Christmas that year my mother bought me a pair of two-power opera glasses, a start anyway. Thus equipped, that May I hiked to a place called Seven Springs and stumbled into the peak of spring migration. A tree full of warblers helped kindle an interest that has never died.

Sometimes I wonder what career I might have followed if Fanny Bronson hadn't been one of my customers.

It was Louis Agassiz Fuertes, whose name is legend in the realms of bird study and bird art, who introduced Fred Garrett to the study of birds:

Somewhere in the mid-1920s "Uncle" Louis Fuertes (to the Boy Scouts he was always Uncle Louis) ran a spring bird contest for Troop 4, in the village of Cayuga Heights, adjacent to Ithaca. The contest ended with a final exam on bird skins in Fuertes's fascinating studio. I flunked the test badly but came out thoroughly hooked on the poetry of bird study, which I pursued, almost to the exclusion of everything else, all during high school. I entered Cornell's College of Arts and Sciences in the fall of 1929 and gravitated immediately to Dr. Allen's weekly seminar.

For Walt Crissey, as finances closed out one career choice, his growing interest in wildlife led to another. In his words:

◆ *The celebrated artist and naturalist Louis Agassiz Fuertes (1874–1927) at work in his Ithaca studio amid specimens and curios from expeditions to three continents. Fuertes was a Boy Scout leader in the Ithaca area, and the local Louis Agassiz Fuertes Council was named in his honor.*

the spring of 1931. I was fifteen years old and a sophomore in high school.

When I was a youngster, my parents emphasized the importance of a college education, and my interest through high school was to go to Cornell and become a mechanical engineer. Money was a problem, but my grandfather, who was independently wealthy, had indicated he would loan me the money. Unfortunately, he died during my senior year in high school and had not made provisions in his will.

By the fall of 1933 I had worked three years on the survey, and Edminster and I had become well acquainted. Knowing my financial situation and my obvious interest in wildlife, Eddie recommended that I enroll in the College of Agriculture. He informed me that he and Doc Allen were in the process of developing a special four-year program in wildlife management. The curriculum had been completely planned, and although it had not yet been approved by the college, both he and Allen were reasonably sure it would be. Following Eddie's recommendation, I entered in the fall of 1933 and enrolled in the

I became associated with the grouse survey in an odd way. Eddie Edminster was recruiting field helpers ($1.50 per day) for the survey and reasoned that members of rural Boy Scout troops might have experience and background that would prove useful. I was a member of a troop in the little town of Enfield, west of Ithaca. Eddie contacted the scoutmaster, who recommended me, and I began work in

A New Curriculum

In mid-1935 a new program in wildlife conservation and management in the College of Agriculture was announced. The five tracks in the program had a common curriculum for the first two years (the courses that Walt Crissey had already taken, following Frank Edminster's advice). For more details about this major innovation, see page 103.

The divisions of the field of wild-life conservation and management as at present recognized by the College are the following:

    I.   Ornithology
    II.   Game-Bird Propagation
    III.   Game Management
    IV.   Economic Zoology and Animal Ecology
    V.   Fisheries

SUGGESTED CURRICULUM FOR THE FIRST TWO YEARS IN ALL FIVE DIVISIONS

FIRST YEAR

First term	Hours credit	Second term	Hours credit
English 1	3	English 1	3
Chemistry 101	3	Animal Physiology 10	3
Chemistry 105	3	Mechanical Drawing 1	3
Wild-Life Conservation 1	2	Zoology 9 (Ornithology)	3
Zoology 1	3	Zoology 1	3
Hygiene 1	1	Hygiene 2	1
Orientation	1	Drill	
Drill			
	16		16

SECOND YEAR

First term		Second term	
Entomology 73 (Aquiculture)	3	Botany 1	3
Botany 1	3	Economics 1	5
Geology 100	3	Entomology 74 (Fish Culture)	2
Entomology 12	3	Zoology 8	3
Zoology 8	3	Elective	3
Drill		Drill	
	15		16

courses prescribed for the planned major. As I recall, wildlife management was not formally approved as a major until 1935. By then I had taken all the listed courses for the freshman and sophomore years. I believe I am correct in saying that two years after the major was established I was the first graduate who had taken all the required courses.

Ben Bradley's route to Cornell was a circuitous one. His father moved to Florida in 1917 and raised beef cattle on a plantation he had inherited from his father. Ben went with him and greatly enjoyed the outdoor features of ranch life. He graduated from Tallahassee High School in 1929 and enrolled in the University of Florida, but he "didn't like it and nearly busted out."

Ben's mother, though, wasn't about to let him forget college, despite his early poor showing. She found out what he needed to transfer to Cornell, and she even enlisted family expertise in French to help him meet the language requirement. The nice part of the story, according to Ben, was that "Mother was living in Spencer, New York, on the farm she had inherited. So little Bennie could drive back and forth to the ag college."

"The Great Depression was still very much there" for Ralph Colson in 1937, when he graduated from high school in Scotia, New York. His immediate idea was to go to work, not spend more time in school, but employment was not without its risks:

I got a job at $15 a week working for a construction company that was building a new studio for radio station WGY in Schenectady at Rice Road, where the old Erie Canal formerly went through. I narrowly missed getting killed twice on that job through accidents and then moved with the same company to White Plains, New York, where I narrowly missed getting killed another time. I decided that construction was not what I wanted to spend my charmed life at. My boyhood interest had been bird study, and I learned of Prof. Arthur A. Allen's courses in ornithology at Cornell, so I decided to apply for admission to the College of Agriculture, which was tuition-free at that time.

Dick Reynolds, characteristically writing of himself in the third person, explains how it made sense for him to go to the College of Agriculture at Cornell:

He was a student from a general farm in rural New York during the early thirties—the depression years—when milk sold for ninety cents a hundredweight and eggs for eighteen cents a dozen. The normal farm workday was fourteen hours. The student had a basic education in the three Rs, with some history and science thrown in. His bird identification included little except English sparrows, robins, and crows. Then he came to matriculate at a college of higher education called Cornell.

Royce Brower supplies this account:

I graduated from high school twice—in Peterboro, New York, in 1926, and Morrisville, New York, in 1927. Peterboro had only three years but would pay tuition to another school for the fourth year. Then on to Morrisville Ag and Tech for two years and to Cornell in the fall of 1929.

So in September 1929 I entered Cornell's College of Agriculture. Of course, the big depression hit in October. Tuition was free then, but most of us thought we ought to eat and sleep and buy books. And there were lab fees. I had $350, so I was OK.

Neal Kuhn was born and brought up in Buffalo, near Forest Lawn Cemetery, where, he later learned, Dr. Allen began his studies in ornithology. "I spent a few summers on the farm in Alden, New York, with an uncle. But my real interest in wildlife came from my father and brother. In fact, I graduated from the New York State Ranger School at Wanakena in the spring of 1937, more or less sponsored by them. From there I went to Cornell in the fall of 1937."

An interest in forestry brought Jim Otis to Cornell. He tells how he arrived at his college decision:

I grew up in Lowville, New York, between Tug Hill and the western boundary of the Adirondacks. One of my best friends was Giles Becraft, whose grandparents ran the Becraft Hotel for loggers at Hoffmeister, on West Canada Creek. He was accepted at the New York State College of Forestry at Syracuse University. I applied but was not accepted. However, I was accepted at Cornell, my father's alma mater. When I got there, in the fall of 1934, I found that forestry was no longer being taught to undergraduates at Cornell.

A political decision had eliminated his major. Instead he studied aquatic sciences and fisheries, and they became his career.

Growing up in central New York, near Oneida Lake—where the fishing was excellent—Chuck Mason learned about game protectors at an early age:

In my circle, "game cops" were the enemy. The game protectors were forever trying to make us boys tag our furbearer traps, limit the number of our ice-fishing tip-ups, and stop shooting ducks and catching spawning pike in the springtime.

When I enrolled at Cornell, I expected to become a teacher of vocational agriculture. However, my informal interest in natural history drew me to Fernow, to McGraw, and later to Stimson Hall. Gradually I reached the conclusion that the brand new fields of fish and wildlife management offered a chance to pursue my primary interest—but on the other side of the game laws.

The new Cornellians arrived on campus with a sense of adventure and a feeling of determination, despite the somber mood of the country in the 1930s.

Arch Petty was three years out of high school in 1934, when his brother Bill (a Cornellian) drove him to Ithaca to make his room arrangements. Arch's first encounter was a memorable one, for they met a colorful Ithaca personality who frequently sang at what she billed as concerts. "Upon stepping from the car at the corner of State and Cayuga, I saw a lady coming toward me to shake hands. In spite of the hot day, she wore a long coonskin coat, and my brother said, 'You've just met Sebela Wehe—a real character.'" (See "The Colorful Soprano," page 6.)

Bill Severinghaus has a vivid recollection of his orientation day:

The orientation program for the College of Agriculture was a lecture in an enormous room with a slanting floor. The professor was way down there behind a rostrum and looked small and far away. I was aghast that there were that many freshmen in school with me. (I found out later that that didn't even include all the freshmen on the lower campus.) I learned from the professor that Cornell was a wonderful educational institution and that I was one of the fortunate few who had the opportunity to be there.

Bill soon signed up for soccer and rowing: "I was tremendously pleased to be in both those sports.

The Colorful Soprano

Morris Bishop, in A History of Cornell, *writes about Sebela Wehe, the singer who made a big impression on Arch Petty when he arrived in Ithaca:*

Miss Sebela Wehe, locally famous dramatic soprano, presented her two-hundredth concert in Military Hall in December 1946. Her shirt-cardboard placards, laboriously written by hand in the Post Office, announced: "She has sang over the Long Distant Telephone to King George, Queen Elizabeth, Marshal Stalin, Gen. MacArthur Tokyo, Gen. Eisenhower, President Truman and Mrs. Truman, who invited her to the White House as a Guest.... Come early and avoid the rush! The early bird gets the worm." Miss Wehe, "the supreme entertainer with the golden voice," was a feature of several Spring Day performances, doing a fan dance. But, as she herself insisted, "Even in my fan dance, I have always been well dressed."

I practiced and played as a fullback at soccer and rowed on the machines in the Old Armory. I did quite well at both."

Once he started attending regular classes, Bill had problems with freshman English, and so did others who had been his classmates in high school in Trumansburg, New York. His uncle Les, who had graduated from Cornell in 1921 with a minor in English, had also flunked freshman English. "So I decided I could live with flunking and do better next year." He made passing grades and received good enough grades in other subjects to act as squad corporal and occasionally as a sergeant during ROTC drill practices.

Art Hawkins's early interest in birds, combined with a growing interest in the out-of-doors, helped him decide on a major in forestry. By his sophomore year, however, Cornell's Department of Forestry was scheduled to move to Syracuse, creating a dilemma for Art and his forestry classmates:

Do we follow or do we choose another career? I chose another career—a decision that led to my first big break. In my major I entered the tutelage of such great teachers as Dr. Arthur A. Allen in ornithology, Dr. Bill Hamilton in mammalogy, Dr. Albert Hazen Wright in herpetology, and Dr. Walter C. Muenscher in botany. Later Dr. Paul Needham and Dr. George Embody provided background in limnology and aquaculture.

Because Neal Kuhn lacked the three years of a foreign language that Cornell required at the time, he had started tutoring with a local high school teacher. The summer before entering college he worked on a dutch elm disease survey in Westchester County. His boss there had a degree in entomology from Cornell. "He talked me into saving money on the French course by getting into the two-year ag program and then transferring later. So when I got to Cornell, I had to take certain ag courses that were especially planned for a farm boy going back to his dad's farm. They were tough for me, but I took all wildlife courses as electives."

Jim Otis remembers himself as "a green small-town boy" standing in line to interview a prospective faculty advisor:

Art Cook from Homer was in line in front of me. We got to talking about possible courses to take. Art was enthusiastic about a new major he called conservation and wildlife management. According to Art, it was the field of the future. That fell right in with advice my dad had given me. "Try to get into a new field," he had said. Art and I both signed up with Dr. George C. Embody, head of fisheries. Art majored in wildlife management, but I stuck with fisheries, mainly because of the advice and counsel of Dr. Embody.

AN ORIENTATION TO THE SURVEY

WALTER F. CRISSEY AND ROBERT W. DARROW

FOR THE GREAT MAJORITY of students who became Hillers, learning about the ruffed grouse investigation and securing an appointment on the crew were largely a matter of luck. Few knew anything about the survey under way on Connecticut Hill before entering Cornell. Where is Connecticut Hill? What was the grouse study? Answers are provided by Walt Crissey and Bob Darrow, both of whom participated in the survey and were among the four authors of the final report, The Ruffed Grouse:

Connecticut Hill is a tract of the Allegheny Plateau located in south-central New York, about fifteen miles southwest of Ithaca. As the investigation contemplated was much broader than Bump's original study, fieldwork was undertaken on a larger part of Connecticut Hill. And since the investigation was to represent the state as a whole, information was needed for regions where the habitat conditions were different from those on Connecticut Hill.

The region most different from central New York is the Adirondacks, and a study area was established on Hale Brook Park, north of Elizabethtown in Essex County, where year-round work was begun in the fall of 1931. Later in the investigation, work was done in other areas, notably in the Pharsalia Game Refuge in Chenango County and in the vicinity of the Alcove Reservoir in Albany County. However, Connecticut Hill was the primary study area throughout the investigation.

By the late 1920s Connecticut Hill comprised land that had been farmed in earlier years but by that time had been largely abandoned. Woodlots that had been cut over were surrounded by old fields that were beginning to fill in with brush. Initially field observations concerning grouse were made on some 2,200 acres of woodland and associated slashings and brush; because they were rarely used by grouse, open fields were not included.

In 1930 Cornell students, most of them majoring in zoology, were hired to make observations, beginning in the early spring. The pattern throughout the investigation on Connecticut Hill was that in the spring a substantial crew worked on weekends, during the summer a small crew worked full-time, and during the fall and winter a limited crew worked on weekends. The number of field-workers ranged from four to six full-time workers during the summer to forty or more during the spring.

The area was divided into sections of 130 to 300 acres that were worked by a crew consisting of a leader and one to four assistants, depending on the acreage. The leader, chosen for his ability and experience, recorded the data. Most of the leaders were Cornell graduate or undergraduate students with training in game management, zoology, forestry, or botany. In a short time a competent leader could initiate inexperienced men into the methods of covering the sections and making the observations.

The work was rugged, and the pay was low ($4.00 a day for the leaders and $1.50 for the assistants). Crews spent an average of eight hours each day, rain or shine, walking through the woods. The terrain was rough, and snowshoes were required when the snow was deep.

Attention was focused on obtaining life history information pertaining to the food and shelter requirements and reproductive success of the ruffed grouse, as well as to the mortality caused by predators, weather, disease, parasites, accidents, and human beings. The crews covered each section 100 percent. The men walked abreast a given distance apart, from one edge to the other, thus covering a strip of the area. Then they went back, covering the

◆ *A view from the Hill toward Seneca Lake, taken in 1941, shows the strongly glaciated and drainage-dissected topography of these uplands. The nearly uniform hilltops reflect the region's ancient status as a high-elevation plateau. By 1941 few hilltop farms remained, and forest was reclaiming much of the land they had occupied.*

Fieldwork on Connecticut Hill began in the spring of 1930 and continued through the summer of 1942. Once the fieldwork was completed, work began on the presentation of the findings of the investigation. To assess the relationships between grouse and the various elements of their habitat, the thousands of field-sheet notations were coded, keypunched on IBM cards, sorted, and tabulated. Records of crop and gizzard contents were analyzed to determine food habits. Autopsy data for collected specimens were assessed for evidence of disease and parasites. Other material pertinent to the physiology of the species was studied, and artificial propagation experiments were carried out. The exhaustive search of the literature was completed. Finally, the graphs and tables were prepared, and the manuscript was written.

That manuscript, discussing the findings of the investigation with respect to habitat requirements of the species and the effects of many environmental factors on the reproduction and survival of grouse populations on Connecticut Hill and in other study areas, became *The Ruffed Grouse: Life History, Propagation, Management,* by Bump, Darrow, Edminster, and Crissey.

adjacent strip, until the entire area had been covered. The end men acted as guides to avoid duplication or missing part of the area. Distances between men varied from sixty to eighty feet during the fall and winter, when the woods were relatively open, to as little as twenty feet when searching for grouse nests in the spring. On average, two men walking fifty feet apart could cover about 150 acres in an eight-hour day. That was a twelve-and-a-half-mile walk for each crew member.

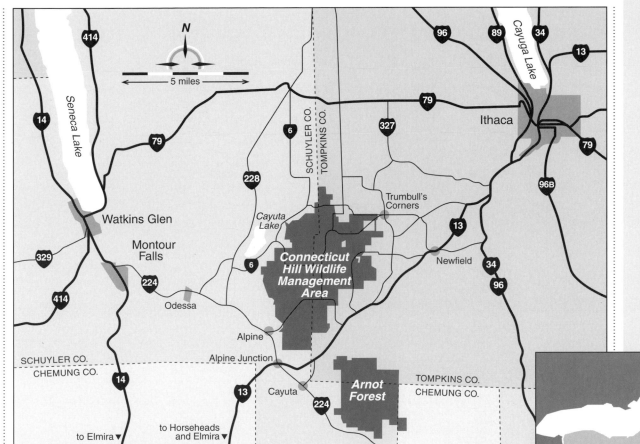

Why Call It Connecticut Hill?

◆ New York State's Connecticut Hill Wildlife Management Area, just south of the two largest Finger Lakes, Seneca and Cayuga. State highways shown bear current route numbers. Also shown is the 4,024-acre Arnot Forest, owned by Cornell University and managed by the Department of Natural Resources as a demonstration and research forest. Starting in 1939, workers from the Civilian Conservation Corps camp in the Arnot Forest participated in the grouse survey on weekdays. (The above map is based on maps from the New York State Department of Environmental Conservation and the Department of Natural Resources, Cornell University.)

In the closing years of the eighteenth century Thomas Livingston purchased a tract of many thousands of acres from New York State. He subsequently sold a third of his land to Robert C. Johnson, a resident of Connecticut. Johnson also bought from the state of Connecticut a large tract in the Western Reserve, in Ohio.

Unfortunately for Johnson, land prices declined, and he owed the state of Connecticut $48,000 for his Ohio land. He was able to strike a deal with his state of residence: Connecticut accepted 16,000 acres in New York in place of the money he owed. Originally known as Saxon Hill, the tract of land became Connecticut Hill, named after its new owner.

Settlement soon began, and Connecticut sent an agent to the scene to handle the land sales. By the middle of the nineteenth century Connecticut had sold off the last of its central New York land.

Prof. Arthur A. Allen conducting an ornithology lab. In January 1930, in this same cramped museum space in McGraw Hall, Gardiner Bump held the first meeting to recruit crew members for the grouse study.

CHAPTER TWO

Openings

LANDING A PLACE ON THE CREW

WHEN THE HILLERS were undergraduates, the College of Agriculture required forty farm-practice credits to qualify for a diploma. One of the appeals of the grouse-survey work was that it could be used for the farm-practice credits. "The nonwildlifers," Don Spittler explains, "had to work out their credits on weekends at the Cornell farm and on private farms during the summer months."

Don continues:

Professor King was in charge of the requirement. Dr. Allen, my faculty advisor, was successful in negotiating with Professor King to permit wildlife students to gain those credits by working in their field.

During our freshman year all students in the College of Agriculture had to appear at the Cornell farm and take a test in such things as harnessing a horse, identifying various types of farm machinery and estimating their work capacity, identifying various breeds of poultry and livestock, and identifying samples of the various farm grains. Fortunately, I identified sawdust in one of the cubicles, and the monitor said: "Very good. You're one of the few that noticed that." Though I hadn't been reared on a farm, I walked out of there with twenty-four points and made up the rest by working on the Hill and spending my summers as a nature study instructor.

That was a real break. I always thanked Dr. Allen for his prowess in the matter, because I checked with several students who worked on farms and learned that Professor King was stingy in awarding points. A summer's work could gain a maximum of ten points, and several students, after toiling all summer for long hours, failed to receive the ten. Many made up the difference by reporting to the Cornell barns on weekends.

Chasing grouse on Connecticut Hill was much more appealing than wielding a manure fork.

It was in Dr. Allen's weekly seminar that Fred Garrett found out about the grouse survey:

I remember Dr. Allen's intriguing announcement, around New Year's 1930, of an organizing meeting for everyone interested in joining the grouse survey. Eddie Edminster and Bob Darrow were probably there, but I didn't know them at the time. I remember the setting for the meeting in the ornithology lab at the south end of the old McGraw Hall museum, which was still largely intact although much dilapidated. The crowd of us were sitting behind the south side of the long worktables in the center of the room with Gardiner Bump on the north side explaining things. I have a clear picture of his rosy cheeks and his impressively precise and measured style of speech.

Ben Bradley wound up on the survey, in a roundabout way, through his involvement in athletics:

Where did Connecticut Hill come into the picture? An odd chance of fate. To keep in shape in the fall of 1930, I did some wrestling. The coach paired us up. My man was named Carl VanDeeman. As we sat resting on the canvas one day, Carl mentioned that a man from the state had told Dr. Allen they were looking for student help in conducting the grouse study on Connecticut Hill. Carl said he

couldn't do it because of a Saturday pomology lab. So—I piped up—how about me? Carl got in touch with Frank Edminster, and he contacted me. As I recall, we had a no-pay dry run in March 1931, and I was assigned to section 9.

The 1930s were difficult times for many. Jim Otis provides a glimpse of that and of his buoyant optimism:

All through college I was short of cash. My dad lost his job as Lewis County agricultural agent in 1936 with three kids in college. I signed up in Roosevelt's National Youth Administration program and got involved in the ruffed grouse survey my sophomore year. It was the beginning of a happy relationship on the Hill. That kind of fieldwork was right down my alley.

Royce Brower didn't work on the Hill until he'd already graduated from Cornell, had several jobs, and then returned to the university. He paints us a portrait of depression-era graduation:

Upon graduating on June 19, 1933, I started for Chicago, where I had a job waiting for me. I pulled a ricksha at the Century of Progress Exposition. The Daggett Roller Chair Company had a franchise to furnish roller-chair and ricksha rides on the fairgrounds. The owner had been a Cornellian and decided to get college athletes to pull the rickshas. I had been on the track and cross-country teams—Coach Jack Moakley had awarded me my "C" as a distance runner.

But after the fair, how to make a living? It was the depression. In June 1934 more members of the class of '34 had jobs than those in my class. I assisted a vo-ag teacher, and in 1934–35 I was an educational advisor in CCC camps. One of the camps was at Arnot Forest, across the valley from Connecticut Hill. The other was near Harrisville in Lewis County. I did farmwork too and whatever other work I could find.

In 1936 I went back to Cornell, as a special ag student—I couldn't afford tuition for grad school. I primarily took courses in biology, in which I had always been interested. That's when I got to be a Hiller.

Sarge Underhill was a graduate student:

I entered Cornell in the fall of 1936 as a Ph.D. candidate. I had graduated from Dartmouth in June, having majored in forest botany and minored in zoology. My committee at Cornell was made up of the famous three: Professors Embody, Allen, and Wright. Doc Allen arranged for me to join the Hill crew that fall, and I worked there most weekends until 1940.

For Lionel Ross working on the survey was a favorable confluence of choice and necessity. He had worked with the Civilian Conservation Corps for

Instructions to Hillers
· · · · · · · · · · · · ·

On January 7, 1938, Harland Fields and Prof. Arthur Allen sent this memorandum to Joe Dell, Don Erdman, Don Foley, John Freese, Neal Kuhn, Bob Laubengayer, and Howard Schuck:

At the end of this month you will be expected to know the Grouse Cover Type Code, and the interpretation of each type, and be able to recognize each type in the field. If you have not already received a printed cover type sheet, do so at once. They may be obtained at the NYS Conservation Department office, 212 Fernow Hall.

Beginning with the first working of the Grouse Survey in February, each one of the above-named persons will work a section of Connecticut Hill with an experienced leader and will be given an opportunity to take field notes.

All the above is preparatory to a job on the state payroll during April and May for each one who satisfactorily passes a quiz on the above work, which will be given on a date near the last of March. At that time you will also be expected to know and be able to differentiate between various animal and bird tracks and any other sign found in the woods.

During April and May while working on the Spring Grouse Survey, you will have an excellent opportunity to learn more about the Grouse Survey, including nesting, drumming, etc., and sometime near the end of May will be given a second quiz covering the entire work. The result of this quiz will determine the amount of Farm Practice Credit you will receive for your work. You are advised that regular attendance is one of the requirements of the credit you receive.

twenty-two months and knew he wanted "some sort of career in the woods. It was enjoyable, and I needed the money desperately."

President Franklin D. Roosevelt appointed many well-to-do acquaintances to leadership positions in his New Deal government at salaries of a dollar a year. Don Spittler tells us how he got his dollar-a-day job:

During my sophomore year (1937–38) I lived in Cascadilla Hall, where I took part in numerous bull sessions in Don Foley's room on the first floor. John Freese, also a class of '40 wildlifer, was a frequent participant. John's major interest was fisheries, but I recall that he did work on the Hill. It was during one of those sessions that I learned about the Connecticut Hill grouse survey, and

Don and John urged me to apply for weekend work. I submitted an application to Walt Crissey's office in Fernow Hall and soon thereafter became a dollar-a-day man.

The tenor of the times provided Don Schierbaum with a practical crash course in economics. After Don received his B.S. degree from Iowa State, in 1938, he sought work with the New York State Conservation Department: "In 1938 the state was broke. Gardiner Bump offered me a job on the grouse survey for $100 a month and then withdrew the offer. He convinced me to go to Cornell for a year and work on the survey on the weekends. During the spring survey I was promoted to leader at $4 a day."

In November 1940 George Elliott was in need of part-time work to finance his stay at Cornell: "Since I was a wildlife-management major, the NYA staff at Cornell said they could provide me a job with the grouse survey. I would be working Sundays throughout the school year. The pay was $16 a month. I grabbed the offer and worked on the Hill Sundays until the third week in May 1941."

Tom Baskous, though not a wildlife student, was assigned to the grouse survey as a National Youth Administration worker: "I suppose I was the only Hiller who was a civil engineer. I worked as a Hiller for two years (1941–42), and it was one of the most enjoyable parts of my four years at Cornell."

Art Hawkins is most indebted to Drs. William Hamilton and Arthur Allen for getting him started as a Hiller:

Bill needed help around the lab, so he hired me under the National Youth Administration program at fifty cents an hour to trap mice, put up study skins, and so on. He suggested that for extra cash and good experience I should work weekends on the grouse survey. I applied, was accepted, and became a Hiller. Dr. Allen may have interceded in my behalf, because by then I was deeply involved in his program.

We were the weekend warriors of the grouse survey, with all the fun and none of the responsibility for putting it all together. What more could one ask?

Ralph Colson was glad to add the survey work to his many on-campus jobs: "Since I was always looking for work to pay my expenses, I readily accepted the offer by the local office of the New York State Conservation Department (Walter Crissey was in charge) to work on Connecticut Hill and the ruffed grouse survey."

Bill Severinghaus gives us a detailed picture of his job placement:

The University Placement Bureau was in Willard Straight in a downstairs room off a hall leading to the parking lot. Mr. Herbert Williams was in charge of student assistance. He was friendly, wonderfully sympathetic, totally helpful and pleased that he could provide the help I needed. I signed up for the National Youth Administration's financial help for students. I had to work for the money. It was fifty cents an hour, 37.5 hours a month, yielding $18.75 a month for eight months (October through May), for a total of $150 a year. I was assigned to a professor to look for reference information in the university library.

About February or March when I got my check, Mr. Williams called me to his office and said that he thought he remembered my telling him that I did a lot of hunting with Dad. He said that a Mr. Edminster was looking for men who liked to walk in the woods for a grouse survey on Connecticut Hill. Did I want to be out-of-doors? Did I have warm woolen clothes? Did I have boots and a jacket for walking in the woods in winter? Yes, I did!

So I went down to Eddy Street to Mr. Edminster's office in his home for an interview. I was accepted and learned I would be working five weekend days each month through May or early June. That meant giving up the rowing practice on weekends, which meant no crew races. I did not want to give up crew, but I did want to get out of that library work. So I took the work on the Connecticut Hill grouse survey.

Walt Crissey was the field crew leader. From the time we left Ithaca until we got back each day was about ten hours. But I enjoyed the time in the woods and being out-of-doors.

The following was summarized from a report entitled "N.Y.A. Student Aid Program at Cornell University, 1935–1936," prepared in the Office of the University Placement Bureau at Cornell.

The National Youth Administration, created in summer 1935 by executive order of Franklin D. Roosevelt, brought work projects to needy youths. The goal was to enable 100,000 students to attend college, paying them for "socially desirable work." Students were selected on the basis of need, character, and the ability to do college work. Colleges and universities could receive up to $15 a month for 12 percent of their students.

At Cornell the University Committee on Placement administered the program. The university established these regulations: the financial aid was to be awarded only to students who wouldn't otherwise be able to attend college; recipients had to be enrolled and carrying a normal course load; and wages were to be fifty cents an hour for up to thirty hours a month.

There were 1,500 applications for fall 1935, from which a list of 654 students deemed most fit and in greatest need was

produced. The state colleges, offering free tuition to state residents, were found to have higher proportions of needy students.

◆ *Herbert H. Williams '26, the epitome of kindly mentors, as we know from Hiller accounts of his thorough, considerate manner of handling National Youth Administration program services. He organized and directed the University Placement Bureau and later became director of admissions and university registrar.*

During 1935–36 about 20 percent of the agriculture students received NYA aid, while only 9 percent of the arts and sciences students and 8 percent of the engineering students received NYA aid.

Work assignments were based on an interview with each student, to match interest and aptitude with available jobs. The arrangement became firm only after student and prospective employer had conferred. Students not only earned money but learned skills and made useful contacts with faculty and staff outside the classroom. About 40 percent of the students did clerical and typing work, 20 percent did maintenance and improvement of buildings and grounds, and 20 percent did either research or classroom preparation. Thirty-three students worked off-campus "in roles of value to state and community." Of those, twelve had assignments with the state Conservation Department's "field game survey."

Payrolls were submitted promptly to Albany so that students could be paid quickly, as many were living from hand to mouth. Almost half the NYA students had additional part-time employment, primarily for room and board.

The celebrated Beaver Bus, 1938. Standing: Stacy Robeson, Glenn Morton, John Schempp, Don Foley, Al Jerome, Norm Jones, Steve Fordham, John Freese, John Whalen, and Don Erdman. Kneeling: Neal Kuhn, Don Spittler, Herb Schrauer, John Morse, Jim Skinner, Walt Crissey, Joe Dell, and Earl Westervelt.

CHAPTER THREE

On the Road

TRANSPORTATION TO AND FROM THE HILL

CONNECTICUT HILL *was an ideal location for New York State's monumental study of the ruffed grouse. Covering more than ten thousand acres, at an altitude of about two thousand feet, it presented an array of habitats attractive to the king of game birds: weedy pastures, hay meadows growing up in brush, second-growth hardwoods, including the essential aspen, and mature timber that had escaped the farmers' axes.*

But how did one get there from the Cornell campus? In those depression years few undergraduates owned automobiles, and fifteen miles to Connecticut Hill was too far to walk. How did the field crews get there? Earl Westervelt remembers that "students were picked up behind Fernow Hall and transported to Connecticut Hill in the Beaver Bus, a vehicle formerly used for transporting live-trapped beaver to new colony sites. Homer DeGraff and Harland Fields were the 'chauffeurs.'"

Walt Crissey, who frequently drove the Beaver Bus, recalls that a number of different vehicles were used to transport field crews from Ithaca to the Hill.

One of the most famous was the so-called Beaver Bus. It was a Dodge truck with an extended wheelbase and a long box on the back without windows. With a bench along each side and one in the middle, it could hold upwards of twenty people. On the way to the Hill in the mornings things were usually rather subdued, but on the way back there was often considerable horseplay. Surprisingly, the worse the weather had been during the day, the higher the morale seemed to be on the way home. One winter day the snow was deep along Ridge Road, and the truck was making slow progress. There was a commotion in the back of the truck (I was driving), and I discovered that John Morse had been divested of his

◆ *Twenty Hillers meet the Beaver Bus behind Fernow Hall.* Standing to left of door: *Bill Severinghaus, Joe Howell, Bob Stein, Kelley Baldwin, Al Bromley, and Carl Lawrence.* Standing to right: *Art Cook, Jim Otis, Walt Crissey, John Robas* (above), *Arch Petty, John Freese, unidentified, Glenn Morton, and two others unidentified.* Kneeling: *Al Wolfson, Dirck Benson, unidentified, and John Morse. Bill Severinghaus recalls this as being spring 1936.*

pants, shoes, and socks and pushed out the back door to run along behind in his bare feet.

Walt recounts how the Beaver Bus got its name:

I was one of those involved when the Beaver Bus was christened. I can't remember the year, but the truck was either new or nearly new, and there was a program to restock beaver in the southern-tier counties. Connecticut Hill was recognized as a logical place, and Edminster had selected a site on section 3N as a suitable location. There was a small stream running through some alder with an aspen grove nearby, and we had built a small temporary dam. Where the beaver came from, I do not know, but they were transported in the Beaver Bus.

Voices from Connecticut Hill

The closest we could get to the site was perhaps half to three-quarters of a mile. Each beaver was in a burlap sack, so we carried them. I suspect mine weighed thirty-five to forty pounds, but by the time we got there, it seemed to weigh a ton. Anyway, as I remember, we released four or five beaver downstream of our temporary dam and gently started them in the right direction. They didn't like our proposed home, and a day or so later several beaver were seen crossing the Ithaca-Elmira Road about eight miles south of the release site. It was hard to say whether they were the same beaver, but there were few around at the time, so they probably were. Later, of course, beaver developed several dams on Connecticut Hill, and one near the road between sections 16 and 17 proved to be a considerable tourist attraction.

Toward the end, the Beaver Bus developed some odd characteristics. The body was obviously built for a purpose other than the one we used it for, and it was not well suited for the rough roads we drove it over. The square body became rather "loose." The driver's seat, gearshift, and brake and clutch pedals were attached to the frame, but the steering column was attached to the dashboard. If you went around a left turn too fast, the upper part of the body and the steering wheel would shift several inches to the right, and vice versa. Needless to say, it was a bit disconcerting.

For the drivers of most cars the dirt roads on the Hill in the 1930s (there are still no paved roads in 1994) must have been a nightmare when wet. Getting stuck, however, held few terrors for the grouse investigators, Walt tells us: "Early on we discovered that if the Beaver Bus ended up in a ditch, it was possible with twenty or so men in the crew to pick it up one end at a time and set it back on the road."

Bill Severinghaus does not remember the Beaver Bus, but recalls instead the Black Maria:

It had a twelve-inch bench along the left and right walls and a back-to-back center bench the full length of the body. It had no windows.

Walt Crissey, Ike Walton, and Homer DeGraff were the drivers I remember. Walt drove a little fast, and on corners we had difficulty staying on the small benches. Ike slowed and accelerated the truck with a hard foot on the pedal. We slid back and forth. And Homer just kept us scared! He had only one good hand, and to shift or turn a corner, he had to hold the steering wheel with his disabled arm. If that vehicle had ever turned over, half of us would have been hurt.

Most nights on the way back to Ithaca, a shoving, pushing, wrestling match would start. Time and again one or more guys ended up on the floor.

◆ *The Black Maria carried not only the Hillers but also a prophetic message from the Bureau of Game, New York State Conservation Department—"Game Crop Is a Community Asset"—echoing President Roosevelt's emphasis on wildlife values in his welcome to the first North American Wildlife Conference.*

On one occasion when we were going down the Hill, before we got to Trumbull's Corners, Homer stopped the truck and announced there was a car in the ditch. About twenty young men got out, stood on all four sides of the car, and at a signal picked the car up and placed it back on the road. Homer yelled, "Back in the Black Maria," and the women from the car stood there beside the road totally astonished.

Walt Crissey recalls a similar event:

On the way to the Hill one morning we were driving along a muddy detour and discovered a car in the ditch with two old couples aboard. (They were at least fifty!) We stopped and asked if we could help, and they said yes. The crew piled out of the bus, picked up the car with the two couples still sitting in their seats, and put it back on the road. I don't think I will ever forget the look on their faces.

For young Hillers like Don Spittler, the first ride to the Hill, in yet another colorfully named van, was one of suspense and adventure:

On the first day of work I raced to Johnny's Coffee Shop (later called Johnny's Big Red Grill), where I bought a bag lunch for twenty-five cents; then off on a run to the rear of Fernow Hall, fearful of being late the first day. When I arrived, Harland Fields was warming up an oversized panel truck. He made a quick head count and yelled, "All aboard!" We piled in the back door and jammed into seats along the sides, leaving a narrow aisle in the middle. Fields slammed the back door and mounted the driver's seat, and the Green Hornet roared out of the driveway between Fernow and the poultry buildings.

The rest of the trip to the Hill was one never to be forgotten. Before we reached downtown Ithaca, the van was fogged with pipe and cigarette smoke, and every time Fields stopped for a traffic signal, exhaust fumes added savor to the reeky tobacco smoke. As soon as we left the city limits, Fields floored the Green Hornet, and at times I wondered if we would reach the Hill in one piece. Some of the old-timers were inured to the hazards of Fields at the wheel, and they dozed off.

Then all hell broke loose! Johnny Morse and Jim Skinner flew at each other, and a wrestling match was under way in the narrow aisle, which was already cluttered with legs and feet. Since this was my first time aboard, I asked the student next to me if he knew the cause of this outburst. "Oh," he said, "They go at it on every trip. We're used to it." As the wrestling match continued, Fields banked to the right, throwing some of the passengers into the melee in the aisle, and we bounded up the dirt road leading to the Hill.

As crews dismounted at designated stations, congestion eased, and the foul air escaped out the back door. Then came my turn to disembark. My name was called by John Whalen, the section leader to whom I was assigned. As my feet hit the ground, I was elated to be on terra firma, breathing clean, refreshing air.

A few years later, when I was in the war in Europe, I often thought that Harland Fields would have made a great tank driver.

Harvey Warner remembers his first day this way:

It was in the winter of 1941, when there was an opening on one of the crews. The first morning that I began work as a crew member, there was about six inches of snow on the ground in Ithaca. Nine or ten of us piled into a vehicle similar to a van, and as we headed up Carter Creek Road, the snow got deeper and deeper. We sometimes had to get out and push. We parked at the caretaker's house, because roads were not plowed farther up the Hill. Snowshoes were brought from the barn.

The Hillers had to be flexible in their expectations and resourceful in the face of adversity, Don Schierbaum recalls:

Transportation to and from the Hill left something to be desired. The first vehicle I remember was the Black Maria. It was a windowless wooden van that swayed back and forth when loaded with the college crew. We had two wooden benches along the sides to sit on. Often we wondered if it would get there and back. Later we got a Chevy suburban wagon. During one spring survey several cars broke down on the Hill, and we returned to Ithaca with all the crew in one vehicle—arms and legs extended out the windows. I believe there were twenty in the vehicle.

Good old 957, a Chevy sedan, rode like a truck. It saw yeoman service. It made numerous trips to Albany for seminars (one a month). No one regretted its demise.

During the war we were unable to buy tires. We were instructed to send all bald tires to Albany for recapping. We never saw them again. Luckily, we had stashed a collection of stone-bruised tires in the cabin loft. We picked out the best and had them vulcanized. The cost was equal to the cost of a new tire. No one complained, and we were able to keep the vehicles operating.

During the summers, when a small crew was living on the Hill, Walt Crissey routinely commuted between work and his home in Ithaca. Joe Dell was one of the live-in crew, and he often rode into town with Walt to get a hot bath, a good meal, and a soft bed:

The first evening I rode in with him, as we approached the end of the ridge to go down the hill toward Newfield, Walt startled me by accelerating instead of braking. We hurtled down a short hill and up another short incline, and as we got just about to the top, Walt said, "Hang on!" As we cleared the crest, all four wheels came off the road and we soared until a solid thump signaled gravity had overcome momentum. When we landed, Walt chortled, "We may have done it!"

◆ *The Boylan house was the field outpost for the ruffed grouse survey, and the seasonal residence for the leader's family and the crew members, during the summers from 1933 through 1936. Its yard was a surprisingly busy parking lot.*

As soon as I coaxed my stomach down from crowding my vocal chords and could speak, I learned that he tried to better his distance record with every trip over that road. And sure enough, he made the effort with every trip I made with him, only then I knew what to expect. The experience gave verification to previous idle comments I had heard from veteran Hillers that Walt was a "Barney Oldfield" (a daredevil race car driver, for those unfamiliar with the name).

Paul Christner had a similar impression: "It was not surprising to me that Walt Crissey became a pilot after driving that Dodge van to and from the Hill. We passengers rattled around in it like marbles in a cigar box."

Arch Petty agrees: "The helpless feeling in that panel truck rocking and rolling and not knowing where you were—it was a sensation duplicated only in an army tank in World War II."

Few Hillers had their own cars, but Jim Otis had a Ford roadster:

It was real handy to carry our four-man crew on the 1936 summer survey to the various scattered sections on the Hill. But hauling four men over the rough Connecticut Hill roads put quite a strain on the car. A rear cross member of the frame broke. Ike Walton went into Ithaca every day. He was obliging and sought out Ithaca's best junkyard for a "new" cross member. Bill Severinghaus and I hoisted the rear end up into an apple tree and removed the broken member. It took a good bit of hard work to chisel off the heavy rivets holding the frame pieces together. The "new" part was fastened to the frame with stove bolts. The old Ford continued to carry us for the rest of the summer.

On a spring day in 1941 Townsend Keeler and John Nemes stopped for a few minutes to write up their observations.

CHAPTER FOUR

At Work

ORGANIZATION, ROLES, AND METHODS

T HE HILL is the New York symbol of wildlife management and the wildlife-management profession. It nurtured the young men who trod its varied habitats seeking information on the life of a prime game bird and learning much more. Few field studies today would enjoy the participation of as many over as long a period. In these recollections the Hillers give us a view of the organization of the work and the people.

Ralph Colson tells us how the day was organized:

We reported early Sunday mornings, rode out to the Hill in the back of a stake-body truck, and got dropped off at our respective sections. Our survey work consisted of walking through the wooded areas at intervals just keeping each other in sight, crossing back and forth and reporting all flushes of grouse. We collected all evidence of predation, such as fox droppings, owl pellets, and feathers from a grouse kill. As crew leader I had to record all information from the crew members on a map for location and in a log for identification. To the best of my recollection, it took about eight transects across our section to complete the day's survey.

Tom Baskous describes the procedure:

We walked through the woods about seventy-five feet apart. We noted the grouse flushed and recorded whether they were male or female. We also noted owl pellets, kills, fox droppings, and so on, and the crew leaders would

R. B. FISCHER

R. B. FISCHER

mark their location on a map. It was so much fun. The woods were lovely, and the men were great company. It was a well-run operation, and work output and morale were high.

R. B. FISCHER

◆ *More than grouse signs greeted the Hillers when they walked their sections. Early wildflowers, like (*clockwise from top left*) bloodroot, squirrel corn, and marsh marigold, were welcome indications of spring.*

Art Hawkins gives us a clear picture of a typical day:

We were provided transportation from campus to the Hill. Once on location we were provided with forms, given instructions on how to use them, and assigned transects to cover that day. Along the transects we recorded everything even remotely involving grouse, their habitats, and their predators. Unforgettable was the pleasure of being in prime grouse country when woodland flowers were blooming and grouse were drumming.

Lunchtime was spent relaxing on a log and enjoying the surroundings. At the end of a long day we turned in our notes and any specimens, such as feathers from predator victims, owl pellets, broken eggshells from destroyed nests, and so on, and were returned to the campus.

Connecticut Hill was divided into discrete study units, and each was given a number. The sections were not always as easy to navigate on the terrain as they appeared on a map, as Don Foley reflects:

We cruised section 16 in late winter. Severinghaus was leader, and Spittler and I were the wingmen. Normally this section was stripped on the contour, but this was one of the times that Edminster wanted it done crosswise to normal. That was often a good idea, but the upper end of 16 is a narrow, steep ravine, and before long all of us were wet and muddy from sliding down one side and clawing our way up the other. I doubt that we saw any grouse while on those maneuvers. We were far too noisy. But it was great exercise.

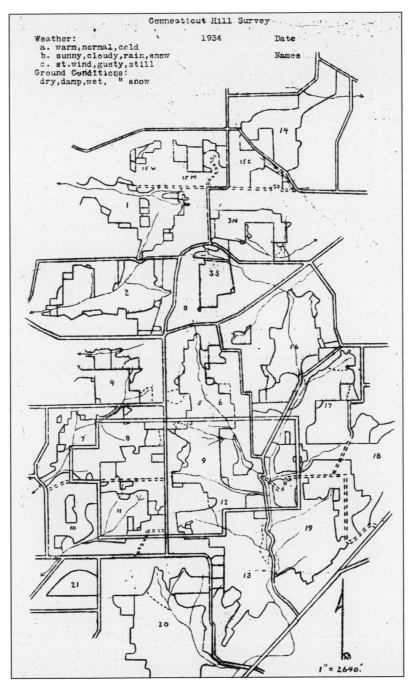

Another time on a section like 16, but not so steep, our crew did the same thing: crisscrossing the main gullies at right angles. When we finally got to the top of the west side after two or three crossings, the guy on my right, John Freese, just collapsed into the grass. He waved me on, and we did the next down and back and picked him up on the next pass. He left the survey and changed his course of study to fisheries. John later became foreman of the DeBruce Hatchery.

Bill Severinghaus explains how the system changed one day:

My sections were 16, 17, and 20. Each had a deep, steep valley with little flatland. Frank Edminster wanted each section worked both north-south and east-west. We had worked them parallel with the valley, and now they had to be worked uphill and downhill. The day we were doing section 16 the two other members of my crew were absent. Frank said he would work, and he had Bob

◆ *A 1934 map of the Connecticut Hill survey area showing the numbered sections. Included in the sections were the areas that were primarily woodlands and brush lots. The map had varied uses, such as plotting the location of predator scats collected along designated roads.*

TONY DeCAMILLO

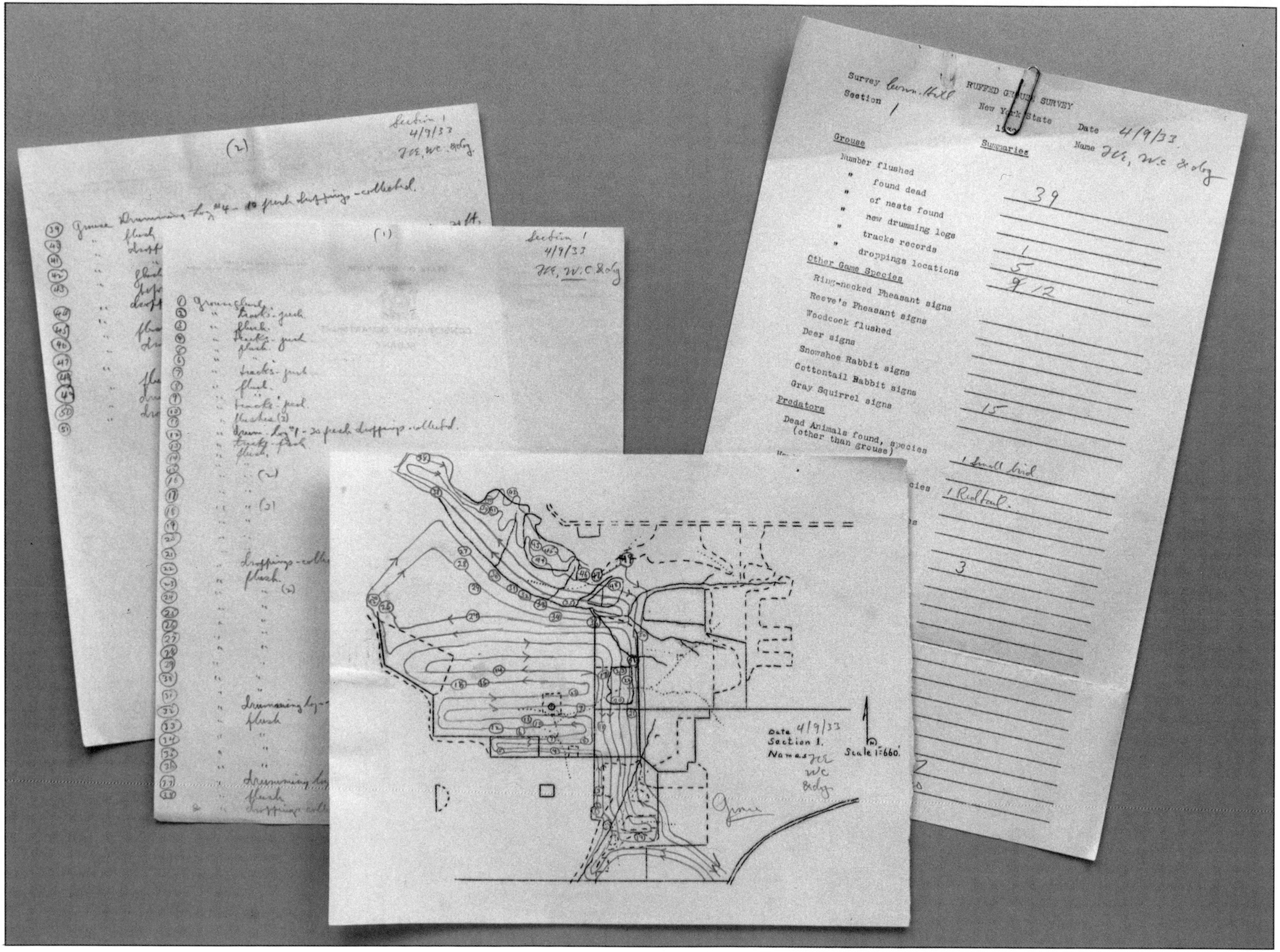

Cameron, caretaker on the Hill, as the second. We started at the upper end of 16 and worked at right angles to the valley. After about six of those downhill-uphill strips, Frank asked, "How much of the section is up and down like this?" I replied, "All of it." He thought for a minute and then said, "This section has to be worked only on the contour."

Next day we were at section 17. It was to be uphill and downhill all day. Frank decided it too should be worked only on the contour. That evening at his office there was a meeting with crew leaders, and he decided, after some explaining by us, that sections with steep-banked ravines would be worked only on the contour. But he wanted us to do our best not to work the same path each week. A decision made in Albany had been changed in the field.

However, Harvey Warner points out that even working on the contour could be tiring: "The first section that I worked as a regular crew member was section 16. Joe Carley was the crew leader. There was a large ravine running through the cen-

---

◆ *On April 9, 1933, Frank Edminster, Walt Crissey, and Frank's dog surveyed section 1. The center map is a worksheet of the section. The crew penciled in the transects and plotted each grouse-related observation, using a number conforming to an entry in the two-page list at left, where all observations were entered serially. On this day they included flushes, tracks, droppings, and new drumming logs. Observations were summarized on the form at the right.*

ter of the section, which meant walking on a steep sidehill most of the day. With luck, one's line of travel would occasionally follow an old logging road, making walking much easier."

The full-time workers, who lived on the Hill, had a long day, as Bill Severinghaus recalls: "We worked as two crews doing routine mapping of grouse flush locations. We had to walk to each section in the morning and back each night. The workday was about ten hours, especially when we went to a faraway section."

While Connecticut Hill was the principal research site, other areas were also surveyed. Bob Darrow was involved both on the Hill and elsewhere: "My direct association with the Hill was actually brief. I was part of the crew, both spring and summer, for the first two years of the grouse survey (1930 and 1931). Then I spent the month of September 1931 at Bump's experimental grouse-rearing station at Harvard, New York, after which I went to Lewis to set up the Adirondack study area."

Earl Westervelt also participated at more than one site:

I spent two years on the summer survey on the Hill. In 1938 I was assigned to the Adirondack survey to take over as leader from Bob Darrow. It was on the Pardee estate near Lewis. Henry Wrisley was the caretaker and my only crew member. Arthur Coonrod was the estate manager and a great historian of that eastern Adirondack area.

No Dickey Birds

Those running the ruffed grouse study made it clear that the Hillers were on Connecticut Hill for one reason only. These were their conditions of employment:

We are running a ruffed grouse investigation; we are not interested in any problems you might have regarding the little dickey birds that flit through the trees, the little bug that runs up the tree backward, the pretty posy that grows behind the third rock to the left of Robinhood's barn, or the interesting-looking snake that wiggles in the grass. You are working for us on our problem while you are on Connecticut Hill; please remember this.

All specimens collected are the property of the state of New York. Connecticut Hill is not a place to build up private collections on any subject. We reserve the right to specify the types of material to be collected.

If you agree to this and the other conditions as set forth, tear off the remainder of this sheet, fill it out, and turn it over to the director of the survey.

There was also a capitol district survey at the Alcove Reservoir. Albany mayor Erastus Corning, a great conservationist, was involved.

The Hillers' recollections provide insights into the various roles performed by participants. Recalling early days of the survey, Fred Garrett focuses on two of the leaders, Gardiner Bump and Eddie Edminster:

My first recollection of Gardiner Bump is that he suddenly appeared as an unknown in front of the group that first day in the McGraw ornithology lab. I wondered where he came from and what his background was. Conversations revolved around what sort of political pull he must have had to land the job. Later, after we all got to know him, the tone changed to commiserating with poor

◆ *Section 9 in 1941.* Top: *It was difficult to stay "on line" in this ravine, whether going on the contour or up and down the slope. Negotiating such terrain on snowshoes in the rapidly changing conditions of a late-winter day was the most difficult.* Bottom: *George Elliott says that just after he photographed this hemlock stand, a grouse flushed from the shelter of the crowns.*

Gardiner, having to spend all his time in Albany pulling the strings that kept the money flowing. Of course, looking at it from this distance, I realize that that was the one job on which all else depended. And judging by the éclat the survey finally achieved, Gardiner performed it splendidly.

Coming to Eddie Edminster, we descend from a godlike figure in the clouds to a very human individual, one of the most effective administrators I have known. The quiet precision of his technique has ever since been an example for me, though I'm not sure how easy it was to copy.

Ben Bradley portrays the character and accomplishments of those two men, the senior leaders of the grouse survey:

In the late 1920s two men planned for and started the ruffed grouse investigation using Connecticut Hill as the prime study area. N. Gardiner Bump got the position as project head, and Frank C. Edminster was his assistant. When Bump moved to Albany to head up the new Bureau of Grouse Control in the early thirties, Edminster stayed in Ithaca in direct charge of the Connecticut Hill operation. The two men conferred often.

Frank Edminster was the leader I associate with Connecticut Hill. He worked hard and set a good example for those of us who were just breaking in. His grasp of the total scope of the grouse investigation was complete. He had a sharp, mathematical mind—and he could write!

Robert W. Darrow was part of the summer survey in 1930, when Bump, Edminster, and the rest camped out in tents not far from the Connecticut Hill cemetery. Darrow labored steadily through the years in this new field of game research and management. Truly an unsung pioneer!

But it was Bump—hard driver and highly ambitious—who was the founder of the state wildlife-management areas we know today. He pounced on the federal Resettlement Administration and succeeded in getting his hands on a number of tracts. His influence changed the rather small Connecticut Hill Refuge of pole traps and buckwheat patches into a managed area. And he saw to it that the acreage was vastly expanded. The records speak for themselves.

Ben describes Gardiner Bump as a hard driver. The following recollection of Bill Severinghaus's illustrates that description:

Ethel Long and I were married in December 1941. When I asked Gardiner Bump for leave time, he approved, and a few days later he sent me a package. In it were five hundred stomach-analysis data sheets from collected ruffed grouse, specific tabulation forms for recording the occurrence of each item in a stomach, a procedure sheet for making a summary of the data, and instructions to have the tabulations completed when I came back to work. We spent the last two days of our honeymoon completing the tabulation and summary.

Jim Otis recalls Frank Edminster as the driving force: "Eddie was the closest contact for work on the Hill. The driving force that kept the project going, he was a tough taskmaster, and everyone liked him."

The head crew leader had an important job. Bill Severinghaus admired the knowledge and ability of Walt Crissey in that role:

Walt Crissey worked on the Connecticut Hill grouse survey during a couple of years when he was in the Ithaca High School. He continued on the Hill while at Cornell. There was nothing about the survey and all of the twenty sections that he did not know. He was Frank Edminster's right-hand man. Whenever there was a problem, Frank would say,

◆ *Section 15.* **Top:** *A mixture of shrubs and hardwood saplings. Just left of center are silhouettes of sumac fruiting heads. Ash seedlings likely are among the invading saplings.* **Bottom:** *The skeletons of dead and dying sugar maples in an old fence line. Just beyond them is a small stand of white pine that is about the height Harvey Warner says could give your face a cold splash when you brushed by in early morning.*

G. B. ELLIOTT

G. B. ELLIOTT

"Walt will show you." He was the leader of the crew leaders, and all of us had a great deal of respect for his knowledge and ability. You could describe to Walt a situation in any section, and he would reply, "I know the exact spot."

When I began work on the Hill with Walt as a crew leader, I was on one end of the line. When the line pivoted on my end, I would time and again recognize something that I had seen on the previous strip. I would tell Walt and add that we were on line. His reply would be something like: "Thanks. I know." So on my pivot I made it my business to check on how accurately he was leading us parallel to the previous line. I was constantly amazed that he knew each section so perfectly that he could lead a two-, three-, or four-man crew back and forth on parallel lines without guidance from the pivot man.

At the end of each day we met in the survey's office room at Frank Edminster's home to summarize the day's observations and make certain our notes were complete and understandable. Checking on us was one of Walt's jobs. Frequently he would ask me a question about the location of an observation, and his description of that location was correct. His recall of field detail was amazing.

One fall day I was called to Ed's office. Walt was there. Ed told us that new cover-type maps were to be made for all the sections. The minimum base area for a cover type was to be a quarter of an acre instead of the full acre of the old maps. (As I remember, there were indications that conifers in a stand much smaller than an acre were a positive influence in the locations utilized by grouse. Therefore the smaller minimum cover-type area was needed.) Walt and I were to do the cover typing. That was a big ego-boosting occasion for me. I would be entrusted to do the same thing that Walt would be doing.

Walt Crissey reminds us that one can get too much of a good thing:

The summer after my freshman year at Cornell I was assigned to a different aspect of the grouse investigation: diseases and parasites. The need was to collect samples of birds throughout the state over a period of years to determine if changes in the incidence of those maladies might relate to changes in grouse abundance. So for the next three years I became a professional hunter—full-time during the summer and part-time during the rest of the year.

The first assigned location was in the Catskills. My instructions were to contact the local game warden, tell him who I was, what I was doing, and why, and ask advice concerning good places to hunt. Early the next morning, much to my surprise, there was a knock at the door of my room, and a committee from the local sportsmen's club, including the game warden, practically rode me out of town on a rail.

From then on those of us collecting grouse told no one what we were doing, and we were never challenged. The assignment drastically reduced the pleasure I got out of hunting for several years after.

Art Cook also found that his specimen collecting was not appreciated, according to Earl Westervelt: "Art Cook worked as specimen collector in the Elizabethtown area. Some of the local hunters were not too happy with his shooting grouse in the summer. He had some slashed tires, way back in the boondocks."

Those who hunt grouse can understand why Sarge Underhill retains this indelible recollection:

Walt Crissey was a phenomenal grouse shot. It seems to me that he ran up a score of over twenty without a miss, and he didn't just take the easy ones. I recall one shot during that string: He tripped over a log just as a bird flushed, and he bagged it as he was pitching to the ground. In those days I felt I was doing pretty well if I averaged one bird out of three shots.

Walt's grouse-shooting expertise was a sore point with Bill Severinghaus: "The first summer I collected grouse, I was told that Walt Crissey collected a hundred each summer, and that was the number by which I would be judged."

It's hard to believe now that students were paid to hunt in the cause of wildlife research. Sarge Underhill says they were trying "to eliminate all birds from cer-

tain sections so that repopulation could be timed and measured." Don Schierbaum remembers trying to remove all the grouse on section 17: "We were able to reduce the population to three birds, or about one bird per hundred acres. We were unable to remove the last three birds. After the breeding season the population was back to normal."

Like other scientific research, the survey work on Connecticut Hill was guided by a standard methodology. But the methods were subject to the vagaries of opinion, weather, luck, rugged topography, and above all a sense of discovery and an excess of high spirits.

From egg to chick to flying grouse—all stages were subject to the scrutiny of the study. Walt Crissey recalls nest surveillances:

When a destroyed grouse nest was found, a determination of the predator responsible was an important element in the investigation. In the beginning there was little specific information available for interpreting the clues that remained around a broken-up nest, and Edminster decided that an attempt should be made to obtain direct evidence. The modus operandi was to build a tree blind near a grouse nest and watch until the eggs either hatched or were destroyed. The blinds were simple platforms about twenty feet off the ground, large enough for a canvas shelter with a clear view of the nest. A light was rigged near the nest with a wire to a battery in the blind in case the female

was disturbed at night and the observer happened to be awake.

Two nests were selected, and Fred Garrett and I were the observers. It was 1932, and I was a junior in high school. With special permission, I took my books with me and studied for final exams while in the blind. My nest was on section 1, and after I had watched for about ten days, the eggs hatched, and the female left with her brood. It was interesting to watch, but what I remember most were the flying squirrels. My blind was suspended on three slender trees, and the platform actually trembled when the squirrels ran up and down at night. They seemed to delight in running across my canvas shelter.

Garrett's experience was different from mine. After about a week he observed a fox approach the nest and flush the female. After chasing the bird for a short distance, the fox returned, obviously looking for the nest. By then, however, Fred had developed a proprietary interest in "his bird." Without thinking about why he was there, he chased the fox away. Needless to say, the fox did not return, and when Edminster found out, I thought he would have apoplexy.

Fred Garrett also remembers that incident, in which a fox paw led to a faux pas:

We had built a tree house blind some hundred feet from the nest of a color-marked grouse. I was taking my overnight turn and awoke at dawn, just in

time to hear the rustle of little feet in the dry leaves directly under the blind. It was a fox heading for the nest. The bird held fast until the fox was almost on top of her and then went off with a great fuss, the fox rushing after her.

Several minutes later the fox was back and, starting about halfway between blind and nest, began systematically working back and forth until it found the nest. At that point my conservative instincts must have taken over. Figuring that we wouldn't want to lose a marked hen with a brood, I watched carefully as the fox's nose slowly advanced toward the eggs, and I hissed at what seemed like the last moment. The fox jumped as if hit with an electric charge and withdrew a few feet, then cautiously advanced again. The procedure was repeated three times (three advances, three hisses), and then the fox gave up and loped off.

When Ben Bradley climbed up to relieve me later in the morning, I blurted out the story as soon as he poked his head over the edge of the platform. I have a vivid picture of his talking head saying: "Eddie will be mad. You should've held off to get an observed fox kill on a nest."

The story has two postscripts. A short time later the nest was destroyed in a way that suggested a fox kill. Eddie never said a word to me about my mistake, but not long afterwards I found out how upset he had been. He had occasion to introduce me to his father, and Eddie Senior's immediate response was, "Oh, this is the fellow who made the awful mistake with the fox." Then, apparently thinking that it was a good opportunity for some fatherly instruction, he said, "Don't forget, any mistake is a mistake of the man in charge." At the time I thought he was wrong. I couldn't see any way Eddie Junior could have prevented my being stupid. But then again, I don't recall any thought of a nest-destruction-identification problem. I had never encountered it. Nor do I recall any formal discussion or briefing about it. Perhaps Senior was right after all.

Vocalization was part of the procedure, but it was also used for fun, according to John Grim:

We would holler back and forth to keep in line, as we were usually out of sight of each other in heavy brush. We had to yell "Flush!" and give the sex of the grouse if we could. Anything like an animal dropping was noted and placed in a paper bag. So were the feathers of a bird that had been killed. Any stranger witnessing those activities would have thought we were escapees from a state institution. Sometimes out of exuberance a crew member would go screaming down a hill at the end of the day just for the fun of it.

◆ *An exuberance of spirit and energy propels Al Hall well over his mark.*

Neal Kuhn remembers that the work even required going barefoot:

When a partridge was flushed, we would backtrack about twenty feet, take off our shoes, and walk a 180-degree arc around the nest. That was to confuse a fox that might be following our trail, of course. Then we would write down all the features, such as the number of eggs, the condition of the

nest, and the surrounding situation, for example, next to a tree, what side of the tree the nest was on, the terrain, the vegetation, and so on. That went on throughout the day, and the crew leader directed and gathered the data.

My time on the Hill was during one of the most critical periods of my life. While my part in the survey seemed ordinary, I was all interest. It was like a pleasant day in the woods. I guess there was a little pay, but that didn't matter. It was a fitting and productive day for me.

Don Schierbaum made some pioneering observations with Walt Crissey in the tandem seats of a Piper Cub airplane:

In 1941 Walt Crissey learned to fly a Piper Cub. At that time we could rent a plane for five dollars an hour, so we decided to survey the Connecticut Hill area from the air. We picked an ideal day: bright sun on a fresh snow.

The deep snow on the hills had forced the deer into the valleys. When flying over section 20S, or Newfield valley, we found fresh deer tracks. We followed them until they went into a dense stand of white pine. After circling several times, we were able to see the deer looking up at us.

Sometimes following the prescribed methods was a tricky business. Bill Severinghaus cites an example:

In May 1937 Gardiner Bump had me collecting eggs from grouse nests. The Bureau of Game needed the eggs to complete the incubation artificially and raise the chicks in order to establish an initial colony of adult breeders. In future years eggs from those adults could be hatched, and the chicks raised and liberated. Someone who found a nest was to call Albany, and within a few days a bureau employee would come to collect the eggs. Five dollars was paid for the clutch.

I was the collector. Gardiner would give me the names, addresses, and telephone numbers of about five people who had found nests. I drove Bump's Buick, in which hot air from the heater was blown into a box that was on the floor of the passenger side. Inside the box were two pails filled with grain. The top pail was for holding the eggs. A long-stemmed thermometer in the middle of the bottom pail showed the temperature of the grain. The temperature was to be kept between seventy-five and ninety degrees Fahrenheit. A higher temperature would kill the embryo more quickly than a lower temperature.

Harvey Warner remembers that in late spring, when the snow was gone, the field-workers moved right on with the next seasonal phases of the survey: "We walked the roads on prescribed routes with a supply of small paper bags. It was part of a fox food habit study, and we were scat collectors."

"To the best of my recollection," Ralph Colson writes, "we always had many paper bags full of feathers and scats, all properly numbered for identification at the end of the day, plus a map showing where each observation or specimen was collected."

Another part of the survey work involved color-marking birds and monitoring their dispersal. The birds that were used had been part of an effort by the New York State Conservation Department to hand-rear the ruffed grouse. Greenleaf Chase recalls the procedure used during the summer of 1935:

Recollections of Connecticut Hill days bring back memories of cleaning the grouse pens at Delmar. Gardiner and Johnnie Bump had already wound up their work with the tired old captive birds. I was to take them to Ithaca, meet Doc Allen and Frank Edminster, and take new orders from there. It was fascinating to watch those two men handle the birds, clip a couple of tail feathers to the quill, and wire on two new dyed rooster feathers of bright red, yellow, orange, green, blue, or white.

Banded and color-coded, the birds were released in uniform color batches on different sections of the Hill. I was to strip-survey each section for a month to check the birds' spread, recording each contact with a host of related data. None of it made much sense to me at the time, but it was my first job in what was to be the most wonderful work— and my career in conservation.

One day in early summer, about three weeks after release, I entered an open glade about lunchtime. While sitting against a stump eating a sandwich, I heard a clucking. A "red-tailed" grouse flew in, landed on my knee, and picked at my sandwich while I stroked its back. Its desire for human contact was so uncharacteristic that I wrote a whole page about its behavior.

Back to Delmar for the month of June, learning to cover-type habitat under the careful training of Ben Bradley. I slept at the Ackerman house on the old floor. No trouble to get an early breakfast of surplus pheasant eggs and be off to our field sites, for Ben was always early. Rip Page, Fred Baumgartner, and I made the daily "school." I remember eating wild strawberries more than the teachings on this experience job with no pay.

In fall we were back at the Hill. Rip Page and Ralph Smith joined forces on my pay of $80 a month. That seemed fair for three people to share a living experience, and we settled in at the Boylan house. The grouse with "colored tails" had dispersed, and we diligently worked the Hill for sightings.

INVESTIGATION FINDINGS

ROBERT W. DARROW AND WALTER F. CRISSEY

BOB DARROW AND WALT CRISSEY, *two of the authors of the "ruffed grouse bible," look back to their days of putting it all together and summarize the findings.*

New York's ruffed grouse investigation had its origin in concern for the future of the species, in light of the extreme scarcity of the birds throughout the state in 1928 and 1929. From the information collected, it was concluded that so long as there is suitable habitat, the grouse will continue to thrive. At the same time, substantial fluctuations in abundance are characteristic of the species. Some additional important findings are summarized here. They must be considered in terms of conditions in New York from 1930 to 1942, when the fieldwork was done.

◆ The abundance of grouse fluctuates in all parts of its range across North America. At the time of the investigation, major declines had not taken place simultaneously over the entire range, nor had recurrent declines followed a regular sequence between regions. Periodic synchronization of the trends of local populations seemed responsible for conditions of general abundance or scarcity within a region.

◆ Failure of the annual increment of young birds was the primary cause of decline in the grouse populations studied.

◆ Food and shelter were the primary factors determining distribution and productivity of grouse populations. Those requirements are best met by a forest habitat in the early stages of succession as opposed to a mature forest with a closed crown, where little light reaches the forest floor. In New York some of the most productive grouse habitats existed where woodlands were broken by abandoned farm fields beginning to revert to woody vegetation—shrubs and trees.

◆ Ruffed grouse were found to eat a wide variety of foods, consisting mostly of plants, although insects were important to the young chicks.

Buds and catkins made up the bulk of the grouse diet, especially in winter, while a variety of fruits and seeds were eaten when available. Food shortages severe enough to cause starvation, weight loss, or death apparently did not occur.

◆ The potential productivity of ruffed grouse is illustrated by the fact that one pair and their progeny would number 33,614 at the end of only five years if sex ratios were equal, all females laid the average number of eggs (twelve), and all sources of loss were removed.

◆ Predation was an important but not critical factor affecting grouse abundance. Rather, it represented a fundamental relationship in the animal community functioning through the removal of surpluses to keep their numbers within limits compatible with their habitat.

◆ The general effect of sport hunting on grouse, as practiced at the time of the investigation, was not detrimental and may even have had a beneficial effect during years of high populations. Much of the loss from hunting was deductible from the overwinter mortality that would otherwise have taken place.

◆ Direct losses from weather were negligible in New York. However, below-normal temperature accompanied by above-average frequency of precipitation during the three weeks following hatching correlated strongly with subsequent higher brood mortality from mid-July through August. It was theorized that the occurrence of those conditions in late spring, perhaps by affecting food supply adversely, produced chicks unable to cope several weeks later with the physiological demands of molting from juvenile to adult plumage.

◆ There was no evidence that disease was important as a cause of periodic fluctuations in grouse abundance.

◆ Artificial propagation of ruffed grouse was found to be possible. Building on the pioneering work of Dr. Arthur A. Allen that greatly reduced losses from disease, means were developed by which a small number of breeding birds were maintained and young birds produced. But the cost was high, and the method was deemed impractical as a means of increasing grouse abundance in the wild.

◆ Although forest habitat in the early stages of succession was determined to be the key to high grouse population levels, management of habitat specifically to favor grouse was seldom considered economically feasible. In most cases, objectives would have to be achieved by integrating beneficial practices with regular agricultural and forestry operations.

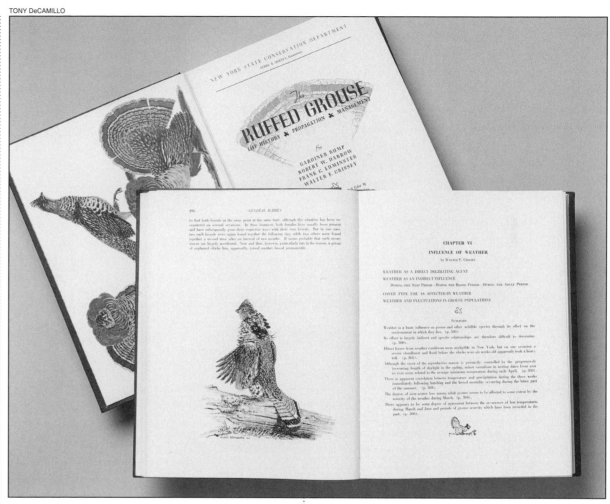

TONY DeCAMILLO

◆ *The classic report that resulted from the laborious work of the Hillers. Replete with tables and graphs and brightened with paintings and sketches,* The Ruffed Grouse *remains the definitive reference after nearly half a century. These opened pages indicate the good design of the book and the illustrations that abound throughout it. The frontispiece, one of four color paintings by Fred Everett, depicts the color phases of the grouse.*

The sketch of the drumming grouse is by Clayton B. Seagears. Together Everett and Seagears contributed 127 sketches to the book. The opening page of chapter 6— "Influence of Weather," by Walter F. Crissey—demonstrates a helpful approach to communicating the complex subjects presented. Titles of the chapter's main sections are listed, followed by summaries of the findings, each with a page number.

Investigation Findings

35

Chuck Mason enjoys a quiet moment of reflection by the campfire during a winter lunch break on the Hill.

CHAPTER FIVE

On Top of the World

SAVORING THE OUT-OF-DOORS EXPERIENCE

WALKING, observing, collecting, recording. That's the way Ralph Colson summarizes his working days on Connecticut Hill. Although his description fits most of a day's activities for the Hillers, they managed to mix in new experiences, a lot of learning, and plenty of fun. "It was an opportunity," says Warren Hewes, "to get outdoors, to walk through the woods and overgrown fields."

Al Bromley, who would many years later become editor of the New York State Conservationist *magazine, was affected by his Connecticut Hill surroundings, as illustrated by these excerpts from his diary:*

October 4, 1937—I am surprised tonight not to find myself exhausted after tramping over Conn. Hill for the first Sunday of this year's survey. Perhaps it was the beauty of the day and the new fall clothing of the hill. Next Sunday the color will be even finer but one couldn't ask for a more lovely contrast of reds, yellows and greens than we found in the clear sunshine of this perfect autumn day. A remarkable incident of the day was the discovery of two "drumming logs" which had been used very recently. One log had over 30 fresh grouse droppings, while the other had about 25. I don't know whether the records for drumming logs would show this to be unique or not. We also saw a junco carrying wisps of dry grass in its bill—purpose? The brushy edges of the woods were fairly alive with robins feeding on choke-cherries and thorn apples. Certainly the grouse cycle hasn't depleted sect. 17 as yet for we flushed a total of 28 birds today; more than I have seen on any one section of the hill for many a day. Deer tracks, droppings, and beds are common on the section. Rabbits seem relatively scarce, as do squirrels. More may be

◆ *A fine, wet snow all day which settled over the bare branches and clogged the pines; ghostly drooping skeletons and sturdy pyramids of white.* —Al Bromley

observed after the foliage is thinner. Blue jays and downy woodpeckers were seen.

November 8, 1937—Worked section 11 today and flushed few grouse—5 in all. It is interesting to note that section 10 which is adjacent to 11, on the South, was heavily populated with grouse

today, 16 being flushed. Working that section (10) last Sunday I flushed only two. Why this migration to section 10? Probably many of them came from section 11. The character of the two are quite different, ten being mostly open field and brushy popple cover whereas 11 is mixed hardwood and conifers for the most part. The day was still and rather warm which might explain the migration to lighter cover. Deer tracks showed up abundantly in the mud and scattered patches of melted snow. One deer was seen. Tracks of one varying hare recorded. Cotton-tails are definitely scarcer than in previous two years. Squirrels also seem to be scarcer judging from tracks. There is a preponderance of grays over reds.

November 15, 1937—After another day on Connecticut Hill. 3N today with Robas and Bagley. The grouse were fairly abundant. Very few rabbit or squirrel were about which lends weight to the observation concerning the wood folks' reluctance to venture out in the early winter snows. It seems quite understandable they should prefer to lie snugly in their dens and burrows dreaming perhaps of sunlit glades than to uncurl their warm feet to prowl in cold, wet snow.

Bob Laubengayer vividly recalls his first day on the Hill: "We covered what seemed like a million miles through briar bushes, broken tree branches, and cutover slashes. Some things you never forget. Needless to say, we all slept well that night. The next day, however, we had to do it all over again in different sections. We soon got in good shape, and with sandwiches and a can of soup, we survived."

Ben Bradley's scores of observations from his many seasons of fieldwork on the Hill provide these glimpses he says have stayed fresh over the years:

- On section 9—My first grouse nest (found two more). Great excitement. Took notes carefully. Did not loiter around the nest site.

- On section 2—Spotted (and recorded) a hummingbird nest on a tree branch.

- On section 1—Came face-to-face with a saw-whet owl as I made my way through a tangle (old tree tops, etc.). We were both startled. I was surprised to be four or five feet from the little creature at nine or ten in the morning. I backed off in an effort not to frighten him (her).

- On section 1—Found a grouse nest where the female had renested. First one broken up. Edminster had "nest-trapped" the female and wired on two colored chicken feathers to serve as positive identification (plus a leg band, I presume).

- On section 4—Discovered a newly born fawn. Its mother had secreted it under a hemlock tree. Light and shade made the fawn about invisible. It did not move. I backed away carefully and

◆ *The high point for me was finding my first grouse nest, in the spring of 1931. I still relive the moment, and my old spine tingles. . . . But whatever the season, whatever the moment, the charm is there—throughout the year—and will remain down through time.*
—Ben Bradley

completed my notes at a respectable distance. That was the first and last sighting. But at that time (1931) deer were scarce (just beginning to filter back after about a half-century of zero numbers). My father in the 1880s and 1890s never saw deer in the Spencer area.

The beauty and appeal of Connecticut Hill were not lost on the young students. Kermit Kruse remembers the early-winter days: "On the Hill my one season, I had the privilege of sloshing through wet snow and also enjoying some beautiful weekends counting grouse."

Harvey Warner responded to the ambience of the Hill:

The Hill had an aura of its own. It seemed clean and fresh in many ways: the pine-scented plantations, washed fresh by rains, each branch ready to douse you with chilled water. The many small streams and occasional springs, most of which were deemed safe to drink. The clouds could be spectacular, and at night the stars seemed brighter and closer.

Cruising a section could mean many different things, as Don Foley found out:

I always remember section 3S fondly, not because it was a small area and could be easily worked by a crew of two or three, but because during spring surveys in May, when it started to get hot, one could always cool off with a drink from the rock-walled spring up in the pines. We never found more than one grouse nest there though. I think it was better winter habitat than nesting cover.

If section 16 looms large in my memory, it's probably because I spent a lot of time there. Besides being big and steep-valleyed, it had some nice scenery, especially down the valley to the

R. B. FISCHER

N. DRAHOS

A. B. BERCHIELLI AND L. T. BERCHIELLI

◆ *Their senses keen, Hillers noted many kinds of wildlife. Don Foley found coal skinks in a shale bank, Ben Bradley came face-to-face with a saw-whet owl, and Art Hawkins found the Hill "a wonderful place to be when the grouse were drumming." Dr. Arthur Allen had a name for that haunting sound: "spring thunder."*

south. Down there near the road was a shale bank, where we most often ate lunch. I remember the skinks (not skunks) playing over the rocks. I can't remember whether I saw one with a blue tail, but I know one lost his tail (with no disadvantage) when we tried to capture him. We were left with a wiggling tail in our hands.

Skinks were also a surprise to Chuck Mason:

One spring day, at a section I will not name, we took a lunch break on a sunny sidehill. My crew stretched out, and pursuing my interest at the time, I started turning over rocks and logs in search of snakes and salamanders. I was amazed to find several coal skinks, a lizard I had never before seen alive. I could hardly wait to report the colony to Dr. A. H. Wright on Monday. Of course he already knew it well. I often wonder if the colony still survives.

The unexpected almost came to be the expected in field experiences. Ralph Colson saw his first flying squirrel on the Hill:

One Sunday afternoon, as we completed the survey on our section, I met the crew leader from the adjoining section on top of the ridge, also finishing for the day. He asked if I had ever seen a flying squirrel. I said no, and he said he knew a tree nearby on the ridge that had a nest of them in it. Picking up a stick from the ground, he led the way, and when he got to the tree, he started tapping on it with the stick as we both looked upward. Almost immediately I saw two small brown objects emerge from far up in the tree and glide down the far slope from the ridge until they both swooped upward to land on the trunk of a large tree and then scamper off out of sight.

I have seen flying squirrels just briefly at night since that time but have never again witnessed such a magnificent daytime performance as I saw that day. Thank you—and if you remember this incident, I sure would like to see you again and shake your hand.

A practice some Hillers used for flushing grouse turned into Joe Dell's first flying squirrel encounter:

During one of the spring-nesting surveys (I believe it was 1940) section 2 was one of my assigned plots. We used a "beating stick" to tap trees, brush piles, and so on, on our line, making noise to flush nesting grouse that might otherwise try to sit tight and let us pass by. As I banged a dead tree, out of a hole near the top sailed a flying squirrel. As is their habit, it glided to a nearby tree, scrambled up to near the top, glided back to its home tree, climbed to its hole, and disappeared.

It was my first sighting of a live flying squirrel. I was so excited and thrilled by the performance that I called in co-workers to share the experience. It was a first for them also. We were all so enthralled that we tapped it out for four or five encores before deciding to desist, lest it abandon its home.

The spring survey consisted of weekly revisits to each section to try to account for all nests attempted and their fates throughout the breeding seasons. For the next few weeks we scheduled our

Dressed for Success

CHARLES MASON

Snapshots taken on the Hill show some Hillers attired in U.S. Border Patrol breeches with a wide stripe, like the ones Chuck is wearing in the photograph on page 36. He provides this information about the garments:

As a land-grant college, Cornell required, at least in the 1930s and 1940s, that all able-bodied undergraduate men complete the basic two-year course of military training (ROTC). At the time the basic uniform consisted of shirt, breeches, and high-cut leather shoes. After service many Hillers put their ROTC uniforms to weekend use. The shoes were soon replaced by more suitable all-weather footwear such as L. L. Bean boots. Later the original breeches would suffer from too many miles of bushwhacking. Their replacement was often a pair of surplus U.S. Border Patrol breeches found at the local army and navy store.

time to arrive at this site for lunch, to again enjoy a couple of flights by our unique friend.

There are many other flying squirrel stories, according to Bill Severinghaus. "One guy," he said, "got bit trying to catch one, and another did get one and kept it as a pet in his room for a few months."

Two foxes put on a first-rate performance for Sarge Underhill:

One spring I observed two red foxes trick and kill a young woodchuck. I was approaching an open field, when I saw a red fox on a stone wall at the far end. He was acting strangely. I sat down behind a tree to watch. He yapped, jumped straight up in the air, then chased his tail. As I looked out over the field, I saw a young woodchuck sitting on his haunches watching the performance. Then I saw the vixen crawling on her belly toward a spot between the chuck and his burrow. When she was in position, the fox jumped off the wall and trotted toward the chuck. He turned and scampered toward his burrow, only to run into the vixen. They killed him and trotted off with their prey.

Many years later, on my farm in New Jersey, I saw my male Chesapeake Bay retriever and my female English setter pull the same trick. The retriever let the setter kill the chuck, getting bitten a few times in the process. Then he took it away from her and carried it home.

A couple of nests caused real excitement for Harvey Warner: "It was on section 16 that I first found a grouse nest at the base of a stump. It was

R. B. FISCHER

W. TRIMM

◆ *Red foxes hunting for a meal were frequently encountered. To see the more secretive flying squirrel, Hillers tapped on hollow trees with sticks.*

an exciting experience, almost as exciting as it was to step into a yellow jacket nest later that year. The ground around my feet was as yellow as spilled cornmeal, and I ran the fastest hundred-yard dash in my life." Harvey also tells us this bee story:

We were working near the southern edge of the Hill one day when we heard a truck stop in the woods a short distance down the hill from us. We felt compelled to find out what they were doing. The truck was parked in a small clearing, and we saw a couple of men carrying something heavy. When we got a little closer, we saw they were carrying supers from beehives. Unwittingly we had moved in too close for comfort. The bees were angry, and they located us. We ran as fast and as long as we could back up the hill. Just as we thought we had escaped and stopped for a breather, Bud Kramer let out a yell and took off again. He had taken his hat off to run and apparently had scooped a bee out of the air and carried it in his hat until he stopped. Then it stung him.

Joe Dell recalls a trick that was played on new Hillers:

It can be a little unsettling when you experience your first ruffed grouse exploding in flight near you, and for several flushes thereafter. You might even flinch. I must admit to having been startled by my first few flushes of grouse or woodcock suddenly popping up from underfoot, but I became acclimated to those surprises after a few days of surveying. At least I quit flinching. Until a new first.

I was working with John Schempp that day and had come out of the woods into a brushy field at the end of one of our cruise lines. All of a sudden there was a loud sound of something whooshing through the air toward me at a rapid rate, and I flinched noticeably. Before I could regain my composure, it was followed by a chuckle so characteristic, it could have come from no one but John.

I later learned it was one of his favorite pranks to move ahead and wait in ambush at a site where woodcutters had produced wood chips (about four by four inches and quite flat). He would throw them with a spinning motion, and they would make the loud sound that had so startled me and others. With his knowledge of the forest cover on the Hill, John was never at a loss to find wood chips when he had a new victim to work on.

Many Hillers remember lunches on the Hill. Harvey Warner tells us about balmy late-spring days: "It was warm work going up and down along the sides of the ravine. When we took a lunch break at the bridge at the lower end of the section, we sometimes took the opportunity to cool off in the pool below the bridge. The air was warm, but the water wasn't."

One spring day Bill Severinghaus had a strange lunchtime experience:

It was a hot spring day on section 17, and I had worked as a doorman at Sigma Phi fraternity the night before until 3:00 a.m. That noon during lunch break I fell asleep. When I woke up, the crew lined up, and I started walking 180 degrees in the wrong direction. Crew members abruptly let me know I was wrong, but I would not believe them. I checked my compass, and sure enough, they were right. I could not understand how it was possible for me to be going a full 180 degrees wrong. So I walked back to the lunch site, saw where I had been sleeping and the direction we had been walking when I sat down for lunch. It was then I realized that somehow while sleeping I had turned my position 180 degrees. For the remainder of the day, I could not get my mind to accept that the direction we walked was correct.

Jim Otis remembers summer lunches: "We would pick up four quarts of milk each morning. One of the crew would leave the milk in the stoned-up spring nearest the section we would be working. Absolutely nothing could compare with that ice-cold milk we would retrieve for use with our lunch sandwiches."

Al Hall underscores that lunchtime often included more activity than just eating lunch:

On a pleasant fall day during the grouse survey, it was not unusual for several crews to meet together at lunchtime. Lunch did not take long. Although

◆ *Jim Skinner, John Whalen, Al Jerome, John Schempp, and Earl Westervelt cool off in the swimming hole between sections 16 and 17 and set up a visual joke.*

Ruffed Grouse Man

DONALD J. SPITTLER

*Don admits that he stole the framework
of this poem from John Greenleaf
Whittier's "The Barefoot Boy."*

Blessings on thee, Cornell man,

Ruffed grouse man, with cheeks of tan!

With thy turned-up pantaloons

And thy merry whistled tunes;

With thy blue lip, bluer still,

Kissed by blueberries on the Hill;

With a grimace on thy face,

Section leader setting the pace;

Record the data as best thou can,

Then back to Fernow in that
low-flying van;

For a dollar a day as a Leopold fan,

I was once a ruffed grouse man!

everyone had been walking over the hills all morn-ing, we were young and full of zip, and soon a touch football game would begin. That was gener-ally followed by a wrestling match—eight or ten

fellows against John Whalen. You could see legs and feet flying, and every once in a while a whole body would be tossed from the pile. Regardless of the number and the odds, I don't remember Whalen ever getting pinned down.

Jim Otis had a lunchtime surprise one day, as Arch Petty records: "During lunch one winter's day (and the lunches were modest and assorted) Jim Otis bit into his sandwich only to find twigs that some prankster had inserted."

Lunchtime during winter was a ritual in its own right, as revealed by Joe Dell's detailed account:

Lunches (each provided his own) while on survey during colder months quickly fell into a pattern most of us observed: a sandwich and a can of soup. We all carried a spoon, a knife, and matches. While one crew member started a fire, we'd cut green-wood forked sticks about three-eighths of an inch to half an inch in diameter and saw with our knife blades around the perimeter of the top of our soup can, leaving about three-quarters of an inch of the cap uncut. We'd bend the cap like a hinge ninety degrees upward, then bend the top third or so back down around the upper fork of the stick. The stick served as a handle for moving the can in and out of the fire and handling it to eat.

Held properly, the lower portion of the stick pressed against the lower part of the can and pre-vented tipping. Timing was important to prevent the green stick from burning through, allowing the

◆ *Arch Petty muses: "Someone talked me into joining the 'bushwhackers,' and the $1.50 a day didn't sound too bad. But at the end of each day on the Hill, when I began patching my tattered clothing, there was some question in my mind."*

can to tip and spill the soup. It was not uncommon for experienced crews to stall their preparations while encouraging first-time Hillers to heat their soup—without warning them to puncture the can. Life is a series of learning experiences.

The midday moments of relaxation reveal much about the fundamental nature of the Hillers. This recollection by Al Hall portrays his crewmates as a generous group:

One wet, snowy, miserable day we were working section 20 with Al Bromley as crew leader. Al never wore a hat, and the snow just collected on his hair and eyebrows. It came time for lunch—we were cold and hungry—so we built a fire. Lunch was often a can of Campbell's condensed vegetable soup, not diluted. That day Al had put his can on the edge of the fire. We all talked, waiting for the food to heat up, and finally it did. Just before Al took his can of soup, someone adjusted a log, and Al's soup was in the fire. His eyes practically jumped out at the fire, and his loss clearly showed. Such a wretched expression I've never seen. However, the crew was generous, and we shared, with the result that Bromley had more than the rest of us for lunch.

Bill Severinghaus remembers another fire mishap:

One day Al Jerome was working with me, a wet snow was falling, and we were wet and uncomfortable. We had built a fire over which we were toasting our sandwiches. Al backed up close to it and was soaking up the heat. All of a sudden, he yelled terribly loud, jumped away from the fire, sat down in the snow, and piled more snow over his boots. He instructed us to take his boots off. Seems his rubber boots had gotten superhot, and steam had developed inside his wet socks at the calf of each leg. The skin was bright red, but no blisters developed.

◆ *Hillers ready to go, after a routine stop for snowshoes at the refuge barn, are John Robas, Walt Crissey, Bob Stein, Red Heidt, Jim Otis, Al Bromley, Carl Lawrence, Paul Kelsey, Kelley Baldwin, and Asa Smith, the driver.*

Winter survey days—seasons when snow blanketed the upper elevations of the Hill—required the use of snowshoes to negotiate the lines. Bill Severinghaus says he was the one to introduce snowshoes to the survey:

During the winter of 1934–35, my first season on Connecticut Hill, there were a few weekends with more than six inches of snow. Dad had bear-paw snowshoes, so he suggested that I use them. That was reported as the first time they were used. Later there was a crust on the snow strong enough to hold my weight, except when I broke through. But such a crust was slippery. So I put two one-and-a-

half-inch stove bolts through the wooden spreader of each shoe, and the slipping was minimized. The next year Walt Crissey bought snowshoes for all the surveyors.

Problems with snowshoe adjustment and even breakage could cause much frustration, as Harvey Warner found out:

Anyone who worked on the winter survey must have had similar experiences with snowshoes.

It helped to get a pair that matched, that had good bindings, that weren't ready to break, that didn't sag too much, that were the right size, and that had a good coat of varnish. Luck wasn't always with us, and we had to struggle with adversity.

When the snow was deep, and you were a couple of miles from the truck, a broken snowshoe could result in a difficult and tiring experience. Most of us could make a quick repair job on the bindings, but sometimes the frame would break in two, making the snowshoes useless. Of course we would try to put splices on the broken frame, but it didn't always work. If the snow had a firm crust, you could use a pole or a crutch and do fairly well. But in soft snow you had to either walk with one foot nearly waist-high and the other plunging to the ground, or you had to take off both snowshoes and wade.

Bill Severinghaus tells us about a snowshoe incident that involved Walt Crissey:

We were working on the north end of section 16. The valley near the bottom was steep, and we were on snowshoes. Somehow Walt slipped, and the tail of one shoe caught on a wood stem and held. Walt ended up head downhill, held by the stem with one leg uphill and the tail of the snowshoe far above his foot. He could not break loose and was hollering for help. I could not see him, so I did not know what he wanted. But I moved his way and saw what the problem was. Without help he would have been there for a long time.

Sometimes the snow suddenly gave way. Don Schierbaum related the time that happened to him and John Nemes:

One day while working on sections 10 and 11, John Nemes fell through the top of a willow tree that grew along a creek. The snowshoes caught on the slender branches, and he was held upside down. The crew pulled him out after a good laugh at his predicament. While still laughing, we separated to get back on our lines, and I fell through the top of another tree with the

◆ *The deer herd was small during the early years of the ruffed grouse investigation, but as the habitat changed, observations of deer tracks and deer beds became more common.*

same results. The crew pulled me out after another good laugh. Neither of us was hurt—just a lot of snow down our necks. We would have had a hard time getting out by ourselves.

Using implements in ways they were not intended is bound to lead to a learning experience, as Al Hall's story illustrates:

One day on snowshoes we were working section 15. The snow was light and fluffy and about twelve to eighteen inches deep. John Whalen was the crew chief. We came to a gully twelve to fifteen feet deep. Most of us went down one side and up the other. John, noticing a tree felled across the gully, decided going down and up was too much. He would use the natural bridge. He did well until about halfway over. Then, not being a tightrope walker, he tipped a snowshoe a little to the right. It proved enough to throw him off the tree and down into the gully. I was the first man to his left. All I remember is seeing legs, arms, and snowshoes flying all over and hearing the most endearing words I've ever heard. They cannot be repeated here.

Bob Laubengayer found he had a lesson in store too: "The biggest lesson I learned was not to try to jump over a wire fence with snowshoes on."

Each year when the snowshoes were taken from storage, what John Grim refers to as a "favorite little pastime" of the season would be revived: "We would stand on the tails of a friend's snowshoes so his first step placed him on his head in the snow. After a while we got in the habit of looking behind before stepping forward. A new man on the crew was always initiated several times before he too began to watch his rear."

Harvey Warner also recalls snowshoe horseplay: "I had seen snowshoes before but had never worn them. There were different sizes and shapes, and not everybody got a matched pair. As soon as some got their snowshoes on, they started trial runs on them. Then the fun began. It was great sport to come up behind the runner and step on the back of his snowshoes to see him flop face down in the snow."

The advent of snow set the stage for other forms of fun as well, like the "snow tackling" that Bill Severinghaus describes:

Sometimes after a day's work there was still plenty of energy to be expended. We would come around a conifer at a fellow Hiller and tackle him, *kerbang,* into the snow! Sometimes it became so general that we all were wet with snow by the time we got to the truck. Once the tackling fun almost caused a disaster.

Albany had called for several hundred pounds of hawthorn fruits. It seems they were to be fed to captive grouse for some test. Ben Bradley was in charge of the eight or ten who spent the day picking the red fruits. He had us fill several cardboard boxes. One was a big shredded-wheat packing box, and Ben was carrying it on his shoulder. It had taken help from others to get it up there.

The tackling game started, and somehow, someone did not recognize Ben and tackled him. I was behind him carrying a much smaller box. As Ben was falling, with his legs held by the tackler, he turned halfway around, holding the box right side up, and fell into the snow. The box came down on his face and shoulders, burying his upper half in the snow, and held him in place. When we picked the box off Ben, he stood up, brushed the snow off, looked around, and said, "That's enough of that foolishness for today."

You should understand that Ben was a well-coordinated athlete—he played baseball at

Cornell—and it was his quick judgment and athletic prowess that prevented the hawthorn fruits from being spilled all over the snow. I don't know what Albany learned from those fruits, but we Hillers picked 'em and got 'em to Ithaca.

George Elliott's memories of springtime on the Hill include snow squalls:

Springtime was especially beautiful on the Hill. It was a great change from the hustle and bustle of the university. I will always remember the quiet serenity, the good companionship, the panorama of the hills. I also remember that walking a straight line in a snowstorm was something else. I worked sections 5, 9, and 15 with John Nemes and Townsend Keeler. Snowshoes were a necessity.

The "day that would live in infamy" occurred on a weekend survey day. Tom Baskous was on the Hill that day: "The event that I remember most was the night of Sunday, December 7, 1941. We had finished our work and gone to a building where we roasted hot dogs for the evening meal. There was a radio there, and we heard the announcement about Pearl Harbor's being bombed."

George Elliott tells us that the Hillers all realized the implications: "Although we spent Sundays during the fall and winter of 1941 and the spring of 1942 on the Hill, we all knew that Pearl Harbor would put an end to survey work for many of us."

±4

#1
23 Oct
1937

Saturday, October 23, 1937
296th Day—69 Days to Follow

Grouse survey #1

Today was cold and it rained practically all day.

I went off on a grouse survey at 8:00 with some other fellows for the conservation department. Four of us tramped through the woods, we flushed a few grouse and got drenched and just about froze. After we got through our stretch of woods we walked to a schoolhouse and built a fire in the wood shed, and gradually dried our clothes and ate our lunches. I burnt holes in my socks in the process of drying, otherwise there was no loss.

The car came for us around 4:00 then I took a hot shower. This evening I wrote a letter to Bobbie.

Sunday, October 24, 1937
297th Day—68 Days to Follow

Today was grey and colder.

This morning, I got up late finished my letter to Bobbie and did a bit of studying.

We had a good duck dinner over at the house which made up for the lack of breakfast.

This afternoon, I studied and then canvassed Baker Tower for the Red Lions Club but didn't meet with any immediate success.

This evening, I went to the chess club and got hauled over the rocks in my first game with a fellow '41. Then I played a beginner for awhile, then Betty.

As a Cornell freshman Don Erdman turned to his diary to describe his first day on Connecticut Hill. His first diary dates back to his junior high school days, and he continues to chronicle his daily activities.

A HILLER'S DIARY

DONALD S. ERDMAN

WHAT WOULD it have been like to walk the sections on Connecticut Hill weekend after weekend? Each day that he worked on the survey, Don Erdman recorded the day's highlights in his diary. In these selections the young diarist shares with readers the Connecticut Hill experience and campus life of more than fifty years ago.

February 26, 1938—Today was fair and cold, but it warmed up later on, and some snow melted. Five of us worked on section 20-S, which is the largest and hardest section of the Hill. It is open to hunting, and we saw two hunters, probably after foxes. We got about 25 grouse flushes and found a dead rabbit. I was pretty well bushed, and I guess we all were when we got through. This evening I just got down to supper about two minutes late, and I certainly did some rushing. This evening I watched Charlie print some pictures and went to bed early.

March 12, 1938—Today was fair and springlike. Three other fellows and I did section 9. There was about three inches of snow, and it got very wet from ten o'clock on. We got more than a dozen flushes in all and saw quite a few woodchuck tracks. At noon we heard some faint honking and looked up and saw about 30 Canada geese high up in the sky, headed north. It was really a thrilling sight. This evening I wrote a letter and did some reading.

March 19, 1938—Today was fair and warm and the best so far this year. Three of us worked on section 2. I flushed a woodcock early, and we reflushed him on the way back. We heard killdeer and bluebirds and saw a flock of about 70 Canada geese and about three red-tailed hawks. There was still a bit of ice and snow in the woods. It got so warm that in the afternoon we shed most of our clothes. I saw a squash bug and, of all things, a caterpillar and other insects coming to life. We did not exert ourselves, so we did not finish the section. This evening I noticed moths around the lamps outside the house.

April 9, 1938—In Ithaca, cold weather and snow. Today was grey and colder. It rained most of the morning on Conn. Hill with a heavy fog. This afternoon it got colder and began to snow with a strong wind. I saw some raccoon tracks. This spring I am assigned with two other fellows to section one. We got about 10 flushes today and saw a woebegone woodcock. When I saw a hermit thrush hopping about the woods, I practically keeled over. We got soaked to the skin in the first hour, and it was miserable all day. When we finished most of the section, we built a fire in the old schoolhouse. This evening I didn't feel like doing much.

April 16, 1938—Today was partially cloudy and mild. Today was good on the grouse survey; we found three drumming logs and one kill. We also heard and saw some towhees and other birds, such as the purple finch. I also saw a woodchuck for the first time in my life waddling up a road. This evening after seeing Walt's young chickens, Walt and another fellow went with me down to Stewart Park, where we found a swamp just outside full of singing toads, peepers, and the low, guttural, scratching call of the pickerel frog. I got one peeper after quite a long wait.

April 23, 1938—Today was fair with little change in temperature. I had a pretty bad cold today; so I felt sort of bushed all day on the survey. We did the hardest part of the section and found several more drumming logs and a fox den in the hollow of a 45-ft. log. There were the skins and feet of two woodchucks, a rabbit, and the various assorted bones lying around the outside. This evening there was the 30th Anniversary Banquet of Phi Theta of Alpha Chi Rho. Five charter members were present, and the total present was 102. There were several good speakers, including Dixon Ryan Fox, Ed Williams, etc.

April 30, 1938—Today was cloudy and colder. It tried to rain now and then but held off nicely until 5 p.m., when it rained quite a bit. Glen found two grouse nests today; 8 and 9 eggs, respectively. We also found a couple of new drumming logs, but we only got four flushes (two birds being flushed off the nest). We also heard and saw a brown thrasher, black-throated green warblers, and a red-tail hawk and nest; however, it was empty. This evening I went to a youth conference in Barnes Hall. Herbert Bohn gave an interesting talk on non-violent techniques in the labor movement.

May 7, 1938—Early this morning it was gray, but it cleared up into a wonderful day. Today I stumbled across my first grouse nest under an oak tree. There were eleven eggs, and the female didn't flush until I was within three feet. We also heard and saw black-throated green and black-throated blue warblers. And I heard several ovenbirds but saw none. Glen also found a nest with 13 eggs. The other two nests now have 11 and 13 eggs, respectively. This evening I took Ted, one of our sub-frosh, up to the rally at Bailey Hall. The Glee Club put on a good showing, and several other fellows and Dr. Day made very good speeches.

May 14, 1938—Today was fair this morning, then it turned cloudy and colder and began to rain around 4 o'clock. I went with Walt Crissey to show him the nests on section one. My nest was broken up by a fox who left no traces. Then I joined Steve. We got quite a few flushes but didn't find very much of importance. This evening I fooled around with a trig problem for two hours, and I couldn't get anywhere so I quit and did something else.

April 9, 1939—Today was my first day of spring survey. There were about three inches of snow on the ground. Stacy Robeson drove us out in the game farm truck, and it was quite a ride. Four of us worked section one; we flushed many birds, though I only happened to see two grouse; but I flushed a woodcock or two several times. I also saw a hermit thrush. Chickadees were present also. The snow was sort of wet; so I got good and wet and cold. Otherwise it was a very nice day. This evening I studied economics and wrote a dozen or more post cards.

April 16, 1939—We found 4 grouse drumming logs, many flushes of grouse, and two grouse kills. One fox had made a temporary den out of an old woodchuck hole. I saw a winter wren, several chickadees; and flushed a woodcock, which walked quite a distance before it flew and whistled away. We found several rabbit kills. There was still quite a bit of snow on the wooded side hills. The trailing arbutus was very green but with no blossoms yet. Deer droppings and fox scats were numerous. One grouse had evidently been drumming on a rock.

April 23, 1939—Today was generally fair and warmer but quite windy and overcast at times. We had quite an eventful day on the survey again and got four grouse kills, several more drumming logs, plenty of fox droppings and owl pellets. We saw a red-tail hawk and several geese which were probably local. We could hear spring peepers even in the early afternoon. Pines sort of gray. I collected lycopodiums and other plants. In guiding I got off the line twice, as I never seem to know too well where I am in the woods. One or two tiny patches of snow were present on the side hills of the deep woods. The tassels of the alders were out, but otherwise there was little new foliage.

13th Grouse Survey
Saturday, March 19, 1938
78th Day—287 Days to Follow
Woodcock flushed

Today was fair and warm and the last, so far this year.

This morning, I went out on the survey and three of us worked on section 2. I flushed a woodcock early and we reflushed him on the way back. We heard killdeers and bluebirds and saw a flock of about 70 canada geese and about three red tail hawks. There was still a bit of ice and snow in the woods. It got so warm that in the afternoon we shed most of our clothes. I saw a squad bug and of all things a caterpillar and other insects coming to life. We did not exert ourselves so we did not finish the section.

This evening I noticed moths around the lamps outside the house.

My essay research starts on the Black Locust
Sunday, March 20, 1938
79th Day—286 Days to Follow

Today was grey and mild.

This morning, I did some reading and studying. Walt came over about 12:30 and we bulled for a while then went over to the house for lunch.

This afternoon, Walt and I went to the library to get material for our library papers. I managed to find quite a bit of stuff on the black locust which is going to be my topic. We saw some swarming honey bees near a tree on the Arts Campus.

This evening I went down to the Methodist church for a meeting of the peace groups.

◆ Don later put tabs on diary pages that referred to Connecticut Hill experiences. The woodcock sketch is believed to be a later addition also.

goshawk. We got several more grouse kills, which means there is quite a bit of predation, though most of it probably occurred in the winter. I saw a carpenter bee buzzing around, and the pink and white arbutus is now beginning to bloom. We got a couple of more drumming logs but no signs of nests. I almost ran into a woodcock, but we couldn't locate any nest. It snowed a bit in the afternoon. This evening I studied economics.

May 7, 1939—Today was fair and as warm as yesterday. This morning we changed to daylight saving, so we got cheated out of an hour's sleep. I got up without much trouble and dressed lightly for the survey. We were thirsty most of the day, though we drank frequently at a spring, and it was quite hot. Black-throated green warblers were singing and field sparrows. We also

April 30, 1939—Today was partially cloudy and sort of cold. Today was a good day on the grouse survey. I heard towhees and saw them, also mourn-ing doves, hermit thrushes, chickadees, ruby-crowned kinglets, and we heard field sparrows singing. We saw a red-tail hawk and possibly a

A Hiller's Diary

saw a white-throated sparrow. Several small bird and more grouse kills were found and another drumming log, no nest, and only three flushes. One of the birds was a mourning dove, and another a hairy woodpecker. The trilliums are just beginning to come out. The number of grouse kills altogether now is about 12. This evening I studied.

May 14, 1939—Today was generally fair and somewhat warmer. It was a good day out on the hill, only I wore low shoes and scratched up my legs pretty badly. I found a crow kill and a grouse kill. We flushed several grouse but found no more nests, except checked up on the nest Bromley found during the week. I saw an ovenbird and a black-throated blue warbler as well as the greens. The trilliums were well out, and the leaves are out but still small. Westervelt found an owl pellet with a hawk's foot inside of it, which was quite a surprise. The ground

TONY DeCAMILLO

was very dry, as there has not been much rain for a long while. This evening I read for my economics paper.

April 13, 1941—Today was partially cloudy but fair. This morning I reported for my first day on the spring grouse survey. Bud Banet drove some of us out in the small Chev. truck. I am working with Roger Bennett on section 11. He is the clip board man, but I guess it was even somewhat new to him. Section 11 is a small section without much bad side hill. There are several good branching creeks for water supply. There was still a little snow in spots under the hemlocks and pines. We got about 10 flushes, and we finished the section. Roger got 5 fox droppings and an owl pellet, and I found what might have been a grouse kill, though only three tail feathers could be found. We heard a hermit thrush singing in the woods, and it certainly was a beautiful bell like song, something like the wood thrush only it does not break off at the end in a lower note. There is good hemlock in the west part of the section, but we found no drumming logs. This evening I read, washed dishes, logged, and went to bed early.

April 20, 1941—Today was partially cloudy and warm with gusty winds. This morning we reached section 11 about 9:00. Roger Bennett didn't have much sleep the night before, so he was sort of tired. Most of the morning while doing the east part of the section we didn't get a single flush. But we probably missed some due to the noise of the wind. We found five drumming logs in all, though 2 were questionable, and one was definitely last year's. I was breezing along when a female grouse flushed out about 10 ft. in front of me. She dropped to the ground and feigned injury near Roger. I looked under the black birch (about 6 in. diam.), and there was a nest with one tan egg. The roots were raised off the ground with the stem, so it was an ideal place and shelter for a nest. The trailing arbutus is in blossom, and popple is in leafy green, and the snow was all gone, but the ground was wet. We got about 8 flushes and most of them in the afternoon. A robin kill, and a couple of fox droppings. We also heard the hermit thrush again. We also got a good sun bask during lunch hour.

May 4, 1941—Today was generally fair and cool. We saw 2 does. Roger and I again worked on section 6. We found a good number of fox droppings and owl pellets but did not get many flushes. We worked close together, found a couple of more drumming logs, but got no sight of a nest. Some trilliums were out this week. This evening our group went out to the Trumansburg Methodist Church to lead a young people's group and a union service. Pep, George, Dick Davis, and Lincoln had gone on ahead. I came on later and picked up Dick Lazarus, who had run out of gas. Dick Davis read the scripture—Matt. 20:17–28, where Christ said to his disciples, "Whosoever will be great among you, let him be your minister." I gave the prayer also and took the text of my sermon from "Blessed are the meek, for they shall inherit the earth." I pointed out that even Christ picked out his close followers not from the leaders of nations but rather good, simple fishermen. Though the total congregation was hardly 30, it was a good service. Lee Burnes asked us over to his house afterwards.

May 11, 1941—Today on the grouse survey it was very cold in the woods for the first hour, 9 to 10, but it warmed up later on. The ovenbird sang with its persistent "Teacher! Teacher!" We saw a magnolia, a black-throated green, and black-and-white warblers. We only got two grouse flushes, however, all day. And only saw one grouse; the other we heard. The trilliums are all out, and they are beautiful.

R. B. FISCHER

In summer 1931 a rented farmhouse replaced the tents of 1930, a change enjoyed by the crew: Ray Tichnor, Fred Garrett, Bob Darrow, Frank Edminster, Ben Bradley, and Pooch, Frank's setter.

CHAPTER SIX

Crewmates

UNIQUE AND MEMORABLE COMPANIONS

*A*BOND THAT WAS TO LAST *a lifetime quickly developed among the students who worked together surveying the grouse on Connecticut Hill. Don Spittler had a term for many of them; they were the "unforgettables."*

"Conventional folks," he says, "conform to generally accepted customs and rarely rock the boat. Each Hiller was a distinct individual. There were no carbon copies."

Fred Garrett sums up the unique social situation that the grouse survey created for the crewmates:

Where else could a tightly knit group of people with common achievement goals, yet highly diverse in personal characteristics except for their generally high level of intelligence, exist in an isolated and unusually pleasant environment that provides ample opportunity for conversation? I think of the flight deck of an airliner crossing an ocean, but few other examples. Our small group was casually together all day long and in three periods of leisure—the morning and evening meals and that jewel of the whole situation, the noon break, where we could satisfy our raging hunger and then stretch out in the shade with nothing to do but rest and talk.

A crewmate Fred worked with six decades ago still stands out in his memory:

In the early spring of 1934 I was on the Hill working exclusively with Fred Snyder, the last remnant of the old Hill families. Anyone who visits the Connecticut Hill Cemetery will notice that something approaching half the stones belong to the Snyder family.

Fred was the most interesting personality I encountered among the grouse survey personnel.

◆ *At a mailbox bearing their names is the 1931 summer crew:* standing, *Ben Bradley, Bob Darrow, Frank Edminster, and Fred Garrett;* seated, *Ray Tichnor. Fred wears the attire that earned him a reputation for toughness in briar patches.*

I can recall almost word for word many of the long conversations we had during the noon break, but I haven't the slightest idea what our work was. He had only a rudimentary formal education but was a gentleman and an excellent friend. He was what I would call a master trapper and was employed as such by the survey. His mind was a treasure trove of woodsmanship, nature lore, and local history. Fred was essentially a poet, sensitive to the nuances of nature and life.

Nick Drahos's cohorts recall Nick as an artist and an athlete. He in turn remembers them in a moment of bright beginning:

I remember lining up at Fernow Hall on the first day of *my* survey in the spring of 1938 with twenty other guys, most of whom became lifelong friends. They included two who would be authors of the grouse book and many others I later worked with in Albany on one job or another.

Bill Severinghaus was known as the bull of the woods. Arch Petty remembers why: "I worked with several leaders, including Al Bromley and Bill Severinghaus. Bill never walked around a blowdown. He would crash through it. I can still hear him yelling through the brush, 'Robas, get off your dead whatever and get going.'"

John Robas is legend in the memories of many Hillers. John aspired to a lucrative career in South America, according to Don Spittler:

IIe prepared for it by taking courses in Spanish on the arts campus. In addition to wildlife, he had a strong bent for forestry and earned the confidence of Professor Recknagel, who gave him a weekend assignment at Arnot Forest. Somehow he also managed to work on the Hill, often to the dismay of his section leader. John had a propensity for making the job easy, and he would often "get lost." Many Hillers should recall the shouts of his section leader: Row-*bass!* Row-*bass!* Everyone knew that John was up to his old tricks. John was also a glib character, well versed in scientific jargon, and he welcomed the opportunity to expound on many subjects. In the spiritual world Robas lives on.

To Sarge Underhill, John Robas was more than a notable character. He was an aggressive entrepreneur as well:

He was young, inexperienced, and not very woods-wise. He was decked out in good Abercrombie and Fitch style: compass, survival kit, emergency rations, and what have you. However, he learned quickly, and despite his youth, he was quite an operator. He soon developed a tree surgery business that put him through college. Later when I was director of fish and wildlife in New Jersey, I knew him as a smart menhaden purse seine captain who revolutionized the industry by developing a gadget that allowed fishermen to set and then close the seine without small boats and haul crews.

As Bill Severinghaus looks back on the summer of 1935, he reports there was only one difficulty—John Robas:

◆ Above: *Frank and Edith Edminster relax with their twins, Stevey and Davey, on the porch of the Boylan house. Edith may be wearing Frank's sweater, adorned with the "C" he earned in 1926 playing hockey for Cornell.*

◆ Right: *Bill Severinghaus retrieved this photograph from an old henhouse, but a mouse had found it first. Bill (shadow) bought Lady from Bill Luce, an Ithaca milk dealer who raised springer spaniels.*

He enjoyed playing practical jokes, and he tried several of them on us. Salt in the sugar bowl, sugar in the saltshaker, and a half-dozen others. It became quite irritating to ruin your bowl of hot cereal in the morning with salt. We threatened him, but it did no good. Jim Otis and I decided to play one on John.

His bedroom was at the end of the hall, and after a bath he would run down the hall, jump for his bed, slide over the blanket on his chest and cover up with the blanket to get warm. Jim and I put a layer of hardbriar stems under his blanket and used up all the hot water so John had to wash with cold water from the pump. He rinsed off with a bucketful over his head and raced for his bed. Landing on the blanket, he slid, and the thorns on the hardbriars laced his chest with bloody scratches. He howled and swore, and we came to see what was the matter. We insisted that each scratch had to be disinfected with tincture of iodine, so we held him on the floor and thoroughly painted each streak. And, oh, how he howled! No more practical jokes.

Briars were part of another Hiller's revenge in this story that Earl Westervelt relates:

Section 17 had a fine spring-fed stream, and if it was lunchtime, the crew would eat and get some sun. Al Jerome was stripped naked and asleep when John Schempp decided to bomb him with specimen bags filled with near-freezing spring-water. Al was so mad he was red, and he chased John a half-mile through blackberry briars. Al had mayhem in his heart.

Walt Crissey had ways to make the job easier on himself, Bill Severinghaus recalls:

With him as crew leader, he had the members of the crew guide off his location. He always guided the line so that he walked the edge of a slashing, and the crew walked through it. One day I asked him how that occurred. His reply: "That's one of the advantages of being a crew leader."

Bill also tells about a difference of opinion he had with Walt: "My Dad had taught me to start a fire using small, dry twigs from inside hemlock branches. Walt preferred the small branches from a white pine. Noon after noon we had a contest to see which fire blazed first, hemlock or white pine. We never did decide, even though we repeated the competition every weekend."

◆ *The Hillers divided up by role and posed. The principals (left): Ike Walton, Frank Edminster, and Joe Howell (Bill Severinghaus wrote on the back of the print "Mandarins of Connecticut Hill"). The crew (right): Bill Severinghaus, Jim Otis, and John Robas (the inscription was "Coolies of the survey").*

Dirck Benson mentions his partner on the Hill, Dick Reynolds:

I don't know what I taught Dick, but from him I learned the local names of trees. As a carryover from California, I knew families and genera. Dick was a marvelous partner, but when spring came, I left the Hill and started wading marshes and following ducklings. I have always envied Dick's

voice—loud and clear—whether he was exclaiming about a grouse nest or a crate of mallard ducklings.

Crew leader Joe Howell receives words of praise from Jim Otis, who calls him one of the nicest men he has ever worked for: "We were a motley crew, but Joe Howell was a real good leader. An ideal field man, Joe had guided A. A. Allen in his search throughout the South for the ivory-billed woodpecker. We had great respect for Joe."

Stories of experiences with Joe Carley and a skunk came from Don Foley, Walt Crissey, Earl Westervelt, and Al Hall. As Don tells it:

Many students were hired to work on the survey. Some lasted; some didn't. One who did was an ag student named Joe Carley. He showed me how to pick up a skunk by the tail—and it worked! He dashed after the critter and quickly lifted it off the ground. The skunk merely looked around unconcerned. After a minute or so, Joe flipped him gently to the ground, and the skunk lumbered off. No spray, no odor, no biting. Of course I never tried it myself, 'cause I figured Joe just might have been lucky.

Earl and Walt both wrote about the time Joe wasn't so lucky. This is Walt's story:

Joe Carley had been bragging that he knew how to catch a skunk in his bare hands without getting sprayed. On the way back to Ithaca, we spied a skunk along the road, and Joe was egged into proving he could do it. The skunk was in some brush, which probably hindered the operation a bit. To make a long story short, Joe was liberally sprayed. Although it was cold that afternoon, Joe rode the running board to town. I never heard what happened when he got back to his rooming house.

Al Hall remembers another time Joe's trick backfired:

Joe Carley was from a farm in Greene County, near Freehold. He was short, husky, and full of bright ideas. He always had an answer. One day a skunk appeared in front of us and wasn't in too much of a hurry. Joe allowed that one should not be concerned about skunks. All you had to do was pick them up by the tail, and then they couldn't spray. He proceeded to demonstrate, and demonstrate he did, proving that his theory was wrong. His prize (or penalty) was the privilege of walking back to Ithaca. However, he still had an answer. He hitched a ride with an old farmer in an old truck. The farmer apparently had plenty of barn on his clothes and in his truck, so Joe's condition did not bother him at all.

Sarge Underhill tells about teaming up with Al Bromley: "I particularly recall how much we enjoyed snow-census work. Bill Hamilton had made us pretty good trackers, and some of the dramas we were able to work out in the snow were fascinating—pairs of foxes hunting grouse and rabbits, grouse roosting under the snow and exploding in a fox's face, owl kills, and so on."

Others also remember Al. Ben Bradley refers to him as "that quiet one." *Jim Otis writes:* "Whenever I was in Albany, I would call on Al. He really made me feel at home. Al had a way of being nice to people." *Bill Severinghaus calls him a memorable crew leader and remembers this experience:*

On one occasion on section 11, the crew stopped while I wrote up a grouse flush note. Then we continued. When we got to the end of the strip at the road, we lined out for the return, but Al Bromley was missing. We yelled but received no answer. Partway back on the return strip we came across a single set of tracks going off at a right angle. Somehow he had moved out ninety degrees to the left after that note stop. I took out after him on the run and found him. He was wondering where we had gone, because he had been yelling and no one had answered. He thought he was ahead of the survey line and that was why he had not found our tracks.

Ralph Colson credits crew leaders Walt Crissey and Don Schierbaum with being "instrumental in developing my interest in the field of wildlife research and management. They gave me the incentive to aim toward this line of work as a lifetime career."

Fred Garrett tells about an incident that illustrates a crewmate's character and reminds us that the depression was a continuing presence during the thirties:

Four members of the survey were returning home in Asa Smith's car from work at another survey site, the Luther Preserve in Saratoga County. A taxi speeding to get a man to the airport on time came around a curve out of control and front-ended them. The cars were destroyed, and the survey members landed in the hospital. When Asa got the insurance money, he gave it to his father, trying to save the family dwelling. They lost the house anyway.

Details of a trip to Detroit in Don Spittler's sophomore year, to go to the North American Wildlife Conference, are still fresh in Don's memory, more than half a century later. The reason: Gordon Leversee, who recruited five wildlife students to share the expense of driving.

Gordie's car was a Hudson or a Nash, and the morning of departure we learned that the rubber was poor. There were several used spares in the trunk, and some were tied to the outside. I can't remember all the passengers, but I do recall Al Groman and possibly John Whalen. All went well

Editorial Note for the Ruffed Grouse Report

ALBERT W. BROMLEY

In anticipation of the survey report, Al Bromley used his lively imagination and quick sense of humor to write a spoof that Bob Darrow calls classic Bromley.

Recognizing the tremendous difficulty in combining in one treatise data which will, at once, be a significant contribution to the biometrically conscious scientific mind as well as a readable and informative volume for John Q. Sportsman, I respectfully submit the following sample as an example of a text which would combine these two apparently violent extremes:—

"Wall, by God, I drug down the old 12 and took me a walk along that thar tote road hopin to get a crack at a patridge fore evnin. You know the road I mean, the one that runs down through that A cover of the south pasture and then up through the B and C cover into the EH with the fine interspersion of types so essential to the complete life cycle requirements of *Bonasa umbellus*. And sure nuff, out got one of the sons a bitches and flew like a danged comet with a corkscrew tail right into a wonderfully located stand of H. Well I let him have it after very carefully computing the standard deviation, using regression by least squares for windage and elevation. But the correction coefficient must have been thrown off by the variance of the difference between means and the whole thing ended

◆ *Al Bromley's fun-loving spirit sometimes carried over to antics on the Hill.*

up as a standard error. You know, I was plumb stumped to find I had missed that critter and I could hardly wait until I could find a nice sunny rail fence to prop up against while I took out my handy vest-pocket Monroe and went right into comparison of individuals and means with a test of significance of regression coefficient, checking with correction for continuity. You'd be flabbergasted to know how I come out, but by this time I was so intrigued that the tobaccer juice was drippin right off my chin into the gears of the machine, and beein Whalen Scrap it sort of gummed up the calclater. So I up with the old trusty once more and headed back where the J combines with the C and A to offer fall feeding grounds at their most optimum. I sure was lucky fer I kicked another one of them things right out from under a brush heap. Now this one must have been watchin the other and had a good memory fer he had the same flyin idears the other had so remembering all them calclations I had run through I just closed my eyes and shot from the hip. Wall, ya know, after peelin off about a quarter of yard of hemlock bark and taking the top clean out of a white pine I still had enough lead left to raise the weight of that thar patridge by anyway a quarter of an ounce. I tell ya fellers, you just can't beat statistics when it comes to ruffed grouse."

until we crossed the Peace Bridge in Fort Erie, Canada. We had just gotten going nicely on the Queen Elizabeth Highway when there was a loud bang, and the overloaded car veered off on the shoulder.

"Everybody out!" Gordie shouted. All the spares tied to the rear and those in the trunk had to be removed to retrieve the jack and tools. With one working and five supervising, we managed to get the car back on four solid tires. "Mount up!" Gordie yelled, and away we went. Chaos prevailed. Before we reached Detroit, we fixed thirteen flats. Our only consolation was the increased ease of unloading, because at each mishap, we tossed another bad tire into the ditch.

There were no credit cards in those days, and we were traveling on a shoestring, but somehow Gordie negotiated for, or appropriated, a couple of good used tires before we left Detroit, and our return trip was less exciting.

About another crewmate Don asks, "Who could forget Don Erdman?"

I can see him now, chugging up Tower Hill Road in his Model T Ford coupe. Don came from the Big City, but his drawl was decidedly rural. He was always cheerful and friendly and phlegmatic to the point of being amusing. His trademark was a pair of Snow-pac boots that he wore throughout the school year. Much of his career was spent classify-

◆ *A sunny day in December 1935 found Bill Severinghaus, Al Bromley, Carl Lawrence, and Art Cook on section 20, where they posed with Bob Cameron, caretaker of the Connecticut Hill Refuge, equipped in the standard manner of the day for his position (varmints beware!).*

ing the fishes of the Caribbean. When we were rounding up the Hillers for a reunion, I called a number in Portland, Oregon, that I had obtained from the Cornell alumni directory. When the party answered, there was no doubt that the familiar drawl belonged to Don Erdman.

Bill Severinghaus has a story to tell about Ben Bradley:

I remember one happening with Ben because it was so atypical. It was sloppy wet and snowing, and we were not enjoying the day. Ben caught the toe of his boot under a root. It held, and Ben fell flat out, full-length, belly down in the sloppy, wet snow. When I heard him, he was damning that root with a blue streak of words. That was the only time I ever heard Ben swear.

And then there's the short-term and nameless crewmate who made a lasting impression on Bill Severinghaus:

One fall a freshman on NYA joined my crew. He continually walked about fifty feet behind the right angle of our walking direction. All the crew asked him to stay abreast of the line. He kept pace with us but always behind. One day as we were walking back to the Black Maria, he walked beside me on the road. "Bill, did you notice anything different about my work today?" "Yes, I did. Today for the first time you walked right abreast with the rest of us. That made it much easier for all of us. Hope you continue next week." "I just wanted to show you that I could keep up with the line if I wanted to. This is my last day on the grouse survey. I've asked Mr. Williams to transfer me to an inside job."

The 1935 summer crew and staff at the Boylan house: John Robas, Joe Howell, Jim Otis, Bill Severinghaus, Frank Edminster, and Ike Walton. The twins are Stevey and Davey Edminster.

CHAPTER SEVEN

At Home on the Hill

MEMORIES OF HILLERS
WHO LIVED THERE

SUMMER 1930: A tent camp provided living accommodations for the members of the survey's initial crew as they concentrated on selecting, testing, and refining methods for their field investigations. "It was set up," Bob Darrow remembers, "where the road from Trumbull's Corners met the Ridge Road. The camp and the crew were under the immediate direction of Gardiner Bump."

In addition to Bob, the crew included Frank Edminster, Glen Chamberlain, and Fred Garrett. Gardiner's wife, Janet, did the cooking, and the Bumps' young son, Bobby, was also there. Edmund J. Sawyer, the wildlife artist, spent some time with the group.

After the first season tents gave way to more substantial frame dwellings, now becoming available as the stranglehold of the Great Depression tightened on a local element of the nation's most vulnerable—farm families struggling to subsist on lands having abysmally low potential to support them, as Prof. Stan Warren's then recent study had described so emphatically (see "Hilltop Homesteads," page 66). At least two different farmhouses served as summer housing.

Bob Darrow was on the Hill again beginning in spring 1931. He has a special reason for recalling the arrangements that prevailed:

In 1931 the summer crew was under the direction of Frank Edminster, who rented a farmhouse near the base of the Hill along the road from Trumbull's Corners. The others were Fred Garrett, Ben Bradley, Asa

R. W. DARROW   R. W. DARROW

◆ *Not only were these young leaders of the grouse survey doing groundbreaking research that would shape their careers, but their families were forming as well.* **Left:** *Gardiner Bump was accompanied by his wife, Janet (also called Johnnie), their son, Bobby, and their dog.* **Right:** *Frank and Edith Edminster, married in May 1929, had a house in Ithaca and kept a tent for overnights on the Hill.*

Smith, Ray Tichnor, and I. After we were married, on July 3, Manda Darrow cooked. Edith Edminster and the Edminsters' six-month-old twins, David and Stephen, were also part of the group.

Ben Bradley's memories of the youngest members of that household are still vivid. With his typical enthusiasm for every moment he spent on the Hill, Ben relates, "They were cute little babies in their cribs in the house at the edge of the Hill where we all nestled in

1931. What a summer!" *In fact, he says,* "I thoroughly enjoyed those two summers." *He continues:*

While we were serious about our work and attempted to the best of our ability to get the facts, there was time for light talk and laughter. Eddie Edminster, knowing that I played baseball on Saturday afternoons with the Spencer town team, was agreeable to my getting away promptly at noon (we worked a five-and-a-half-day week). My trusty 1930 Ford Model A made it all possible. And I reported back to camp each Sunday evening ready to work Monday morning—sometimes with bruises from sliding on not-too-smooth diamonds.

When summer 1932 rolled around, Ben was on the crew once again, and very busy. With the Darrows now in northeastern New York, where Bob was setting up the grouse investigation's Adirondack study area, Ben found himself doing much of the cooking and food buying. Perhaps related to those indoor obligations is his memory that "Edminster had a portable record player (a Victrola) with a good assortment of records (of course we had no *electricity). One record was a thing about two warriors—Abdul Abull Bull Amir, and Count Ivan Skavinsky Skivar. Both died fighting."*

Fieldwork continued to hold Ben's interest, but not to the exclusion of leisure time and its lighter moments, such as the incident he calls "the discus episode":

I got the idea that I needed to strengthen my arms and upper body. The discus might be just the ticket. I bought a "practice" model and practiced alone. Then one day I wanted to show the summer crew my prowess. In the field across from the house it happened as the audience watched with bated breath. I spun and let fly. Not a bad throw but a bit off line, and the nice new discus landed on a stone wall and shattered. You see, the practice model was made largely of cast iron.

By the year Bill Severinghaus joined a summer crew—1935— the first farmhouse had been given up for the Boylan house, a site admirably central to the study area. Bill remembers the strong family orientation of all the occupants that summer, complete with exemplary housekeeping habits by crew members in deference to the Edminsters' impressionable sons:

R. W. DARROW

R. W. DARROW

◆ Above: *The mess tent, ornamented with a grouse in the star up front, was Janet Bump's domain as she cooked for the crew that first summer. Some of the paraphernalia present was required for Bobby's care.*

◆ Left: *Manda MarLett, Bob Darrow's fiancée, who had just graduated from Fredonia Normal School and found a teaching position in Jamestown, visited him at the tent camp during the summer. They were married early the next summer, after he graduated from Cornell.*

Frank Edminster, his wife Edith, and the twin boys—Davey and Stevey—stayed in the same house with us all summer. The field crew did all the dish washing and housecleaning, and we had to be neat, clean, and orderly as a good example to the twin boys. So we had to wash our clothes a couple of times a week, because our work was hot and sweaty. And we had to wash our own sheets. Water was heated by the sun in a tub on the ground, and the clothes were hung on a line to dry.

Bathing that summer was an experience. We had a big washtub on the front porch roof. Each morning it was filled with water from the pump in the yard by filling a pail, pulling it up with a rope, and

Hilltop Homesteads

. . . .

STANLEY W. WARREN

In May 1927, when Professor Warren was a student at Cornell, he wrote a report on Connecticut Hill. This is an excerpt from that report.

This region comprises 7,300 acres of sub-marginal land. It has been settled for about a hundred years. The father of Mr. Arno Snyder, one of the present residents, came here with his father in 1829. The original settlers came in from the north, and instead of stopping in the fertile hardwood region around Cayuga Lake, they came on to this hill region because the timber was better (white pine).

The population increased until about 1875, when competition from the Midwest began to be felt. In 1926 there were thirty-seven people living in the region. There were thirteen occupied farms, seven of which were operated. There were ninety-three homesteads at one time.

Tillability is questionable, but two-thirds of the land was cleared, and over 30 percent was farmed at one time. The land is assessed at $9 per acre. Most of it could be bought for $5 per acre.

◆ *After a summer in tents the Hillers had farmhouses as their summer residences:* top, *in 1931 and 1932 a house on the road from Trumbull's Corners;* bottom, *from 1933 through 1936 the larger and better-located Boylan house.*

. . . .

dumping the water in the tub. The water was in the sunlight all day long and was warm by afternoon. We got to the roof from a second-floor window, and before supper we washed there and then dumped a pail of water over ourselves to rinse off the soapsuds.

Bill recalls that the crew was able to eat well, albeit inexpensively:

Frank had each of us pay seventy cents a day; he paid seventy cents each for himself and Edith and fifty cents each for the two boys. Frank bought all the food and brought it from Ithaca each day. Hamburger was a dollar for five pounds, and bread was ten cents a loaf. We had milk for breakfast only. We did a lot of berry picking that summer after work on our way home, and those berries were frequently our dessert after supper. We also ate a lot of them as we picked. Several times we shot a woodchuck, and it was dressed, cooked, and eaten for supper. One Friday night at the end of August, Frank drove all of us to Newfield after supper, and each member of the crew bought and ate a quart of ice cream. His family had ice cream sundaes.

Breakfast was always cooked cereal, and lunch was sandwiches. Peanut butter and apple butter were common ingredients. We occasionally had pancakes with brown sugar and sausage for supper. Hamburgs and meatloaf were common, and there were always plenty of potatoes and fresh vegetables. Mrs. Ed cooked supper every day, and we ate regularly at 6:30. She often said it was fun to cook for us, because we ate anything and everything that was put on the table.

Among Bill's other memories from the summer of 1935 were evening games, a ferocious storm, and Edith Edminster's classical piano music—on request, live:

Monopoly was the rage that summer, and we played after the dishes were washed and the table cleared. Most of us played every night.

One night at the farmhouse we had a terrible thunderstorm that was centered around us. One bolt hit close, and the flash and kerbang came together. Next morning we discovered that the iron wire that stretched between two maple trees, on which we hung our wash, was melted off the trees, and burn marks showed where the wire had encircled the trunks.

Somehow Edith Edminster arranged to have a piano at the house, and she would play when she wanted to and when we asked her to. A graduate of the Ithaca Conservatory of Music, she was a concert pianist and a piano teacher.

Greenleaf Chase spent some of his leisure time trapping: "I had my first fox-trapping attempt 'by the book'; I caught a weasel in a stump set and a horned owl in a pole trap. We kept the owl in the woodshed and fed it mostly scraps and rats. It consumed seven rats one night. The woodshed was between the kitchen and the outhouse, often making the crossing a scary one at night."

From tents to vacant farmhouses to a cabin of their own, centrally located on Ridge Road—that was the evolution in living accommodations experienced by Hiller summer crews during the first eight

◆ *For almost the last half of the survey, 1937–42, summer crews enjoyed this new and unique facility, a cabin built of American chestnut logs. "Memories of living there are cherished by many of us," says Walt Crissey, survey leader during those years.*

years of the survey, 1930 to 1937. The cabin was no ordinary one, but one built of American chestnut logs salvaged from nearby woodlands, where scattered dead trees, whether standing or fallen, remained sound years after the fatal fungus that killed the trees had swept through the state's central counties in the 1920s. The high tannin content of the chestnut wood served as a remarkably effective natural preservative. While many readers might not recall that tragic loss, the rapid progression of the fungus and the extent of its damage resembled the widespread mortality in American elm during the 1960s.

Bill Severinghaus describes the cabin:

There was a room of double-decked bunks, a living room with table and chairs, and a kitchen with a woodstove. On the long wall of the living room was a three-foot-high and three-foot-wide stone-faced fireplace. The caretaker had cut and piled plenty of wood outside the kitchen door for the stove and the fireplace. A couple of us had sleeping bags, and the others had blankets.

Bob Laubengayer remembers "a beautiful cabin with all the conveniences, a bucket to bathe in, a fireplace to dry by, and so on."

The cabin builders had all requisite skills except one: fireplace construction. When a crew of six students (Paul Christner, Art Cook, Al Jerome, Gordie Leversee, Jim Otis, and Bill Severinghaus) settled in on December 18, 1936, to conduct grouse surveys during their two-week Christmas recess, the flaw immediately became apparent. Paul Christner describes the first remedy they tried:

The only source of heat, other than Chef Severinghaus's cookstove, was the fireplace. It smoked like hell, which activated six youthful brains. It was decided that raising the fire level would solve the problem, so flagstones were collected for that purpose and duly installed. Then a rip-roaring fire was started, and we relaxed to enjoy our smoke-free environment. Hit the deck! Shrapnel began flying as the rocks warmed up and exploded. A preview of things to come.

By Bill Severinghaus's account, their efforts the next evening brought more success, if less excitement:

The fireplace smoked terribly, because it was not deep enough and was too high; but mostly because it had been built without a smoke shelf. The second night we cut and split a chestnut log about twelve inches in diameter. With nails and refuge wire, we hung half of that log, flat face toward the stone, so that it lowered the top of the fireplace opening about 10 inches. This reduced the smoke coming into the room by about 90 percent. With the stove and fireplace there was plenty of heat, but every morning the cabin was cold, because we made no deliberate plan for getting up and fueling the two fires.

Bill goes on to provide glimpses of their experiences at the cabin during that typically wet, cold season:

Al Jerome had brought along a pet blue jay that he kept in his room at Cornell. It had the freedom of all three rooms in the cabin. The first evening it flew to the kitchen stove and landed, and with a loud squawk it flew off (hot feet). At breakfast and supper meals, it would walk about the table picking up bits of food. When we were in camp, it would fly

◆ *The first reported use of the cabin was a survey during the 1936 Christmas recess. The crewmates who participated were Al Jerome, Paul Christner, Bill Severinghaus, Art Cook, Jim Otis, and Gordon Leversee.*

about, sometimes landing on someone's head or shoulder. Once it flew out the door, and we caught it when it landed on someone.

Inside the cabin we had strung several lines of refuge wire from wall to wall. Most days we were wet, and each evening the six of us had to hang our field clothes, including our underwear, over the wires so they could dry. Moving about the cabin among all those hanging clothes was hazardous.

For recollections of the cabin's primary use as living quarters for summer crews, we turn first to Walter Crissey, an occupant the initial summer season—1937:

One incident I recall had to do with root beer. Homemade root beer was popular in those days and rather inexpensive (which was an important factor). Somewhere we had obtained eight one-gallon jugs with corks, enough for a double batch. Since it was warm in the loft over the bunk room, we put it up there to "work." About the second day we discovered that all the corks had blown out. We reinserted the corks and then carefully inverted the jugs, setting each one on its cork, and carefully wedged them so they wouldn't tip over. When we returned the following afternoon, we discovered that all eight jugs had broken, and the mix, which included several pounds of sugar, had leaked through the floor of the loft onto our beds and the floor below. Although we mopped repeatedly, it was several years before bare feet would not stick to the bunk room floor on a humid day.

Bathing facilities at the cabin were limited. They consisted mostly of a bucket of water for each man, which we left out in the sun to warm during the day, followed by buckets of rinse water from the spring— all of which was accomplished in the side yard. I remember that the springwater was really cold. It was fun to watch someone else cringe when you threw water over him, but it was not so much fun when it was your turn.

A problem during the early part of the summer survey many years was money—no one had any.

We turned in a payroll at the end of the first month, but it was usually another two to three weeks before we got the first checks. Fortunately, I had an uncle in the grocery business in Ithaca who was willing to finance us and also sell us staples at wholesale prices.

Bob Laubengayer mentions Walt's uncle as well: "We had no money to buy food, but good old Walt Crissey came through again and got his uncle to trust us till the end of the summer. By that time we owed more than we had coming in pay."

The job of cooking that summer fell to Walt:

We didn't have fresh meat too often, but with milk from a local farmer at three cents a quart, plus berries and an occasional pie or cake from home, our food bill averaged less than eight dollars per person per month. I usually ended up being the cook, and there were few complaints, not because I was a good cook, but because whoever complained got the job.

Earl Westervelt doesn't remember objecting to the cooking: "A quite common dinner was five pounds of rice, soaked all day, and a half dozen cans of Campbell's chicken soup with wild leeks or onion.

◆ **Left:** *This photo of Bob Laubengayer, which he captioned "mopping up," shows a spick-and-span cabin interior and the handsome log partitions.* **Right:** *At horseshoes Bob concentrates on his aim as his opponent, George Nazaruk, looks on apprehensively.*

During blueberry season there were lots of blueberry pancakes, muffins, pies. Those who had homes in the area would have their mothers bake the pies. They were real good."

Al Jerome's pet crow was an integral part of cabin life that first summer, as Walt Crissey relates:

I remember the incident of the .22-caliber ammunition and the pet crow. There had been a flood in 1937, and a case of .22 ammunition (five thousand rounds) had ended up underwater. Some would fire, some would not, and some would fire after a

fraction of a second. Anyway, I obtained the ammunition as a gift and took it to the cabin. We placed a target on a convenient tree and shot from the front porch. This was the summer that Al Jerome found a young crow that had fallen from a nest. He raised him as a pet, and he became tame. Unfortunately, we must have fed him the wrong things (bread and milk, as I remember), because the flight feathers never grew properly, and he could not fly. The evening we shot target we left the empty shells scattered on the porch and the ground outside. The following evening, however, there were no empties to be found. The crow had carefully picked them up and stuffed them in cracks and holes around the cabin. For years after, empty .22 shells could be found in the strangest places.

The crow developed a character of his own. There was a pine tree next to the cabin, and he discovered he could hop up through the branches and jump to the cabin roof. When we returned in the afternoon, he was glad to see us (hungry, perhaps) and would launch himself from the end of the roof. He would hit the ground with a great thump and roll end over end. Although he never seemed to get hurt, he did seem angry with himself. He would get up, dance up and down, and caw loudly several times before running to be picked up.

Late that summer someone brought several bottles of beer to the cabin, and I think it was John Schempp who discovered that the crow liked beer—so much so that in short order he was obviously drunk. Schempp thought it was funny, but Jerome became incensed over the way "his" crow was being treated. I am pleased to report that the crow showed no signs of a hangover the next morning.

Earl Westervelt also remembers the tipsy crow:

There were wild poker sessions at the cabin after supper. Someone who had been to town would bring back 3.2 beer for the games around the Aladdin lamps. One night someone thought Al Jerome's pet crow should have beer. The crow liked it poured into his beak, and he got real tipsy with much loud cawing. He was hilarious, and so loud he awakened Al, who came from the bunk room totally naked and mad as hell at us for having taken advantage of his crow. It was real humorous watching Al try to get the bird to stay on his perch outside the window in his (the bird's) inebriated condition.

Earl writes about other pranks that the crew members perpetrated on each other during the course of the summer:

On rainy days we worked on the bound volumes, recording all the data in india ink. Walt Crissey had

a "hot" date with Martha one night, and we decorated him like an Indian warrior. It took three to hold him down while two decorated. It must have been quite a date.

Jim Skinner worked on the summer survey, and he slept on a cot outside the bunk room. When Jim snored, it shook the whole cabin. One night we took a tube of Burma-Shave and gave him the big squeeze. He came up looking like a mad dog. Luckily, he could not pin it on any one of us.

John Schempp had some firecrackers that he had saved for an "occasion." In the middle of a hot night he lit a string and dropped it from his upper bunk to the floor. That cleared the room, and the cabin, for the rest of night.

Wayne Trimm learned one night that peace and quiet can be difficult to find out-of-doors as well:

I remember a time I had to sleep on the Hill and bunked down near the cabin in my sleeping bag. In the middle of the night I was jolted awake. A large raccoon had landed on my chest. As my eyes snapped open, I found myself looking into the face of the masked intruder, about five inches away. For some reason it just stared at me and didn't move. I managed to get my hand out of the sleeping bag, for it wasn't zippered closed. Then, as quietly and quickly as possible, I grabbed the animal by the back of the neck and threw it off to my right with more than my usual strength. The last I heard of the raccoon was its crashing through the brush.

Bob Laubengayer's summer crew even managed a fishing trip to Canada at season's end: "We were supposed to work twenty-five days a month and take the other days off. Our group decided to work fifty days straight and go to Canada fishing the last two weeks."

Joe Dell's first summer in the cabin was in 1939, and he describes his summer home: "The state-built cabin on the Hill had no electricity, so our kitchen stove and lamps burned kerosene. Our water came from a spring. The springhouse served as a refrigerator. An outhouse was our bathroom." *That summer, as Joe recalls, the crew's wildlife companions were two fledgling red-tailed hawks, Chief and Champ:*

My first summer I slept in one of the bunks until the night we were awakened by a muffled explosion followed by a sticky liquid dripping on me and soaking the bed. It turned out that a few days before I arrived, Al Jerome had made and bottled a fresh batch of root beer and was aging it above my bunk. That incident plus some resonant snoring in the bunk room convinced me to move to a folding cot near the fireplace. The next morning the young red-tailed hawks that Jerome was "mothering" started screeching at daybreak for their breakfast. They regularly roosted on the chimney top, and their cries were amplified as they came down the flue. In later years I often wondered why we hadn't brought the hawks indoors and let them hunt their own breakfast. Our resident population of white-footed mice would have sustained them for many weeks.

Because of the remote location of the cabin, we did not have ready access to butchery by-products or roadkills to feed the two fledgling hawks, so occasionally we had to use a .22 rifle to shoot wildlife. One evening when it was my turn to hunt, I shot a red squirrel near the camp. As I went by the horseshoe court adjoining the cabin, the players engaged me in conversation. Too late I caught the sound of flapping wings and almost at the same time felt some pain in the hand that had been carrying the squirrel, now gone. That was the first time either hawk had come for its food without being coaxed. Previously they wouldn't come in until we placed their food on the ground. Luckily a talon had only grazed one of my fingers, but from then on we stayed vigilant when bringing food into their visual area. As I recall, both birds left to forage for themselves not long after the incident.

Harvey Warner entitled his varied recollections of summer 1942 "The Last Summer":

We lived at the cabin, which was in good condition. There was the large stone fireplace in the living room, assuring a pungent odor of smoke. The bunk room had two double-deck bunks, and the loft overhead could accommodate several more people. On a clear, sunny day we aired the mattresses. We hauled them up on the cabin roof and left them there during the day while we worked a section. There was running water in the kitchen, piped in from a springhouse. There was also enough water

◆ *On a summer day in 1942 Grace Warner, Harvey's mother, delivered baked goods to the crew, a gift they welcomed, for, according to Harvey, they did no baking.*

in the cellar below the trapdoor to make a reasonably good refrigerator. There was a porch across the front of the cabin where Richard Kramer hung a hand-carved sign, "Bohemia Hall."

Five of us lived in the cabin that summer: William Burke (crew leader), Bud Kramer, Wayne Trimm (I'm quite sure), and Douglas Cox. Paul Kelsey lived in a tent about a hundred yards away from the cabin, and if I recall correctly, Kenneth Beck commuted from Newfield, though he may have stayed at the cabin too.

A few things stand out as memorable. Paul Kelsey, who was on the Cornell track team, liked to work out early in the morning. Occasionally some of us would jog along with him about a mile up the road toward the old cemetery, then run back to the cabin. For a while we'd nearly keep up with Paul, then about halfway back he would pick up speed and leave us in the dust.

One Sunday afternoon John Doll and I took a shovel and flashlight and went to explore the old coal mine we had heard about. The entrance was closed down to the size of a woodchuck hole. We dug it open enough so we could crawl in. We could see water in it, but we didn't know how deep it was. When we eased ourselves down into the water, we were relieved to find it came only to our knees. We found the shaft was only about thirty feet long and six feet high. There were black rocks along the sides but nothing that looked like usable coal.

Evenings were relaxing. Lots of talking, sometimes card games or reading. About three times a week we bought milk from a farmer near Trumbull's Corners. It was nearly two miles each way, so if we didn't get a ride, it was a long walk.

Someone brought boxing gloves to the cabin, and occasionally some of us would "square off" if we still had energy to burn.

All of us on the crew in the summer of 1942 knew it would likely be the last of our carefree days for quite a while. The war had already started, and we savored each day we spent on the Hill.

A Cornell scene the Hillers knew well. The building with the tower is McGraw Hall, the first library, which opened in 1872. During the era of the Hillers it housed natural science classrooms and collections.

CHAPTER EIGHT

On Campus

WORKING, STUDYING, AND PLAYING

ATTENDING CLASSES, *studying, and working kept the Hillers busy, but they had fun too. They went to football and baseball games, and they participated in those sports and many others. They stopped in at Zinck's and Leonardo's and found time for parties and dates. Their biggest problem was paying for room and board. They had many jobs, traded services for food, and even picked up cafeteria leftovers.*

When Ralph Colson came to Cornell, he was totally on his own. He arrived on campus, in September 1939, with only $300 saved up:

I had no other source of financial support, since both of my parents were deceased. I was starting a new adventure but with lots of courage and determination. My first objective after enrollment was to find work, and I somehow found a job waiting table at a fraternity house (where male students with adequate financial support lived).

This job gave me sustenance, which was of primary importance. An exchange of work for food—that simple—but good food, I must say. I never went hungry a single day of my four years at the fraternity house (three years as head waiter, which meant more responsibility but took less time).

One of my part-time jobs was working for an entomology professor, caring for and dissecting cockroaches at forty cents an hour from NYA funds. I learned more about insect anatomy on that job than in any course I ever took.

Another job was cleaning rooms of rich students and in one case just getting rid of the trash. It included dirty cooking pots and utensils, dirty clothes, and other trash among valuable items

◆ *According to Don Foley, an April day in 1939 found most of the conservation majors in the class of 1940 gathered near a dairy barn that had experienced a fire. They are John Freese, Earl Westervelt, John Schempp, Lionel Ross, Al Jerome, John Whalen, Norm Jones, and (in front) Al Hall.*

such as cameras, skiing gear, expensive clothing, jewelry, and so on, strewn all over the floor. I couldn't even walk across the room without stepping on something, so I just threw up my hands and walked out. That was the only job I ever had while at Cornell that I refused to do.

Neal Kuhn had to earn his room and board all through school:

I got a job taking care of the furnace for Mrs. Blood in Cayuga Heights and walked back and forth to campus. I worked in fraternities for board, especially Delta Chi, where I had a high school friend.

The summer before my second year at Cornell I worked on the dutch elm disease survey.

The following summer I got a job on the state game farm in Varna raising pheasants under Dick Reynolds. It was a wonderful summer. I learned a lot.

What does it mean to be lucky? Here's what it meant to Royce Brower:

I was lucky enough to get to live and work in what was known as the ag boarding house in Forest Home. It was just down the hill from the dairy building and the dairy barns, across the street from the schoolhouse. I stayed there two years, waiting table, washing dishes, and mopping floors.

And my luck continued. In the second term of my sophomore year I was invited to join Alpha Zeta fraternity. At that time a member could earn his room and board there by waiting table, washing dishes, and so on. With that and student loans from the NYS Grange, plus summer jobs, I made it—albeit with loans to repay.

Don Spittler learned some out-of-the classroom economics managing his meal tickets. He recalls:

The Great Depression had a profound effect on the money we had in our pockets, but price adjustments in the marketplace could transform a little bit of dough into a lot of bread. Some may remember the meal tickets that were available in many of the Collegetown restaurants—as I recall, they sold for $7.50—and with frugal management they would carry a student for a week. I remember economizing through the week and splurging on Saturday evening, when I would feast on a T-bone steak with all the trimmings at Johnny's Coffee Shop for seventy-five cents. Hamburgers were a dime at most places, and a huge vegetable plate at the Eddygate Restaurant was only thirty-five cents.

The $8.00 Don Schierbaum earned each weekend as a crew leader paid for his room and board. He spent $3.00 for room rent and $5.00 (worth $5.50 in food) for a meal ticket at Johnny's.

Looking back at fast (and cheap) food in 1938, Arch Petty said that his daily wage of $1.50 as a Hiller "did come in handy and bought many gallons of skim milk at the dairy building at five cents a gallon, which together with two pounds of Fig Newtons for twenty-five cents, would suffice for a meal."

Mason Lawrence lived at home in Brooktondale during both his undergraduate and his graduate years. He spent most of his spare time working to pay his school expenses. "When I had a little extra time, I attended athletic events and lectures."

◆ *Sometimes Hillers went deer hunting in the Adirondacks. That's where this party was in November 1934. Walt Crissey scored, as did Ben Bradley, then a busy emissary for Gardiner Bump. Those gathered in Inlet were Vic Skiff, Frank Edminster, Walt, Ben, and Bob Darrow.*

His farm background gave Paul Christner an edge in earning some much-needed money while having a good time:

In the fall of 1935 Professor King employed me as one of the examiners for farm practice—long since discontinued. To this farm boy, it was a real treat to see how many ways a horse could be harnessed: collar upside down and face forward, harness over the rump rather than the shoulders, and the breeching over the shoulders. What an education!

Someone took a chance and hired me the following summer to work at the game farm—its first year under Dick Reynolds. It was the most

fun-filled summer I ever spent. Pheasants were raised then in brooders and also in the field with mother hens. But just try to grow a bird with tail feathers in a brooder house!

There were two brothers in charge of field birds, and I was on the brooder bird detail. While there was no competition regarding who grew the best birds, I made, or tried to make, a case for brooder birds. Any time a sleek cock with ample tail feathers was presented to me, I used it as evidence that brooder bird rearing was best. What fun that provided!

Sometimes their food sources didn't supply balanced meals, but they did provide interesting diets (witness Arch Petty's skim milk and Fig Newtons). Art Hawkins writes about an arrangement he and other students of Dr. Allen had with the cafeteria run by the College of Home Economics:

The Allen students were a close-knit group. Several of us ate lunch together in McGraw Hall, the main entrée being a peanut butter sandwich. Some of us went through Cornell powered on peanut butter, and I still like it.

Leftover food at the home economics cafeteria was ours if we were there to pick it up. If the class exercise for the day was desserts, our leftovers that

◆ Above: *It looks cold enough to freeze a smile on Al Jerome's face.*

◆ Right (clockwise from top): *Fernow Hall, the campus head-quarters for the grouse survey. The building was so crowded, even in the late 1930s, that Al Bromley didn't have space for his long legs. Bill Severinghaus was destined to return to this Fernow room to lecture many times, but few remember him in a sport coat; his usual attire was north-woods wool.*

day might be seven kinds of desserts to go with our peanut butter sandwiches. One time the home ec classes made brown bread, and dozens of loaves were surplus to their needs. We salvaged all the loaves we could carry and stored them in a box on the fire escape outside a second-story window of McGraw Hall. Toward spring some of the loaves got a bit moldy, but only on the outside, and it was easily trimmed off.

Art also used his rabbit-hunting skills to extend his meal ticket at Harry's Diner, near where he lived: "Harry liked to eat rabbits, and I liked to hunt them. I got twenty-five cents' credit for every cottontail I brought him. Maybe that made me a market hunter—that didn't occur to me at the time."

Part-time work under the National Youth Admin-istration program was a boon for Chuck Mason, and not only because of the money:

The highlight of my job was finally being assigned to the zoology office. My primary tasks were to work with the collections and to maintain W. J. Hamilton's mailing lists for the Ecological Society (he was the secretary). The out-of-class associa-tions with W. J. Hamilton, A. H. Wright, Ed Raney, and their teaching assistants greatly enriched the course work in vertebrate zoology.

Hillers write a lot more about working than play-ing in their accounts of their college days, but there were lighter moments. Paul Christner remembers when three classmates from his high school in LeRoy, New York, came to campus:

They had no money but were anxious to see a foot-ball game. We joined a sizable group back of the Crescent on a fall Saturday hoping to find a way in. The sliding doors collapsed under pressure but yielded a dead end. Let me emphasize that the LeRoyans did not contribute to the pressure but, being familiar with sliding barn doors, did offer to help the campus cop prop them up—from the in-side. We were then acquainted with a way to get in and saw the game.

To Ben Bradley getting two letters in baseball was a dream come true. Recalling Cornell baseball, the Hillers' star of the diamond shares these other highlights:

What was the most thrill-laden incident with the ball nine? It had to be the headfirst dive across home plate to snatch a 1–0 victory from Harvard in 1933.

The most vivid event had to do with our exhibition game with the Cleveland Indians. Walter Johnson was the manager, and he pitched three innings, easy like. So I had a time at bat—grounded to the ss. A part of the game.

A pet great horned owl belonging to Al Hochbaum, a fellow advisee of Dr. Allen's, was the center of unexpected attention in an incident Art Hawkins witnessed. The owl frequently stayed in the studio of George M. Sutton in McGraw Hall:

George was the talented bird artist in residence, and Al, who later became a famous waterfowl biologist, was an avid student of Sutton's techniques. One day Al was walking across the quadrangle not far from the studio with the owl perched on his shoulder. Suddenly the owl took off and landed near the top of a giant elm. For some reason the inexperienced owl tipped over when it landed and hung upside down, afraid to let go. The fire department was called and finally rescued the owl with the aid of a long ladder.

Ransom Page tells a story with a romantic ending:

Greenie Chase was my co-worker on the Hill. He and I wanted to go out on the town one weekend. As Greenie was new to the Cornell campus and did not know anyone to ask, I got him a blind date. It went so well that Greenie ended up marrying her. He is now retired as a wilderness wildlife specialist and lives in his beloved Adirondacks on Ampersand Bay, Saranac Lake.

Greenie fills in some details about his blind date:

R. B. FISCHER

One afternoon Rip Page asked me to join him on a blind date that evening with his girlfriend and the unknown. Many hours later Rip drove us to a diner on the edge of campus. The two girls and I went in for coffee, and when we came out neither Rip nor his car was there. Giggling, they pointed me across campus to the fraternity house where I was staying. I tried to hush them as we pushed my old Model A out to the road and quietly coasted off to a start. Thus I met the girl of my dreams, with whom I shared a glorious life.

These reminiscences from Don Spittler give credence to his reputation as a fun-loving guy:

COURTESY OF B. O. BRADLEY

◆ Above: *Ben Bradley, first baseman on Cornell's varsity nine, as he appeared in his uniform the month of his graduation, June 1934. He received varsity letters in 1933 and 1934.* Left: *A great horned owl, like the one Al Hochbaum had as a pet, the one that had to be rescued from a tree.*

One of my frequent companions at the movies was Dwight Webster, who continued his graduate studies at Cornell and made his name in the field of fisheries. There were several movie houses downtown, and admission was twenty-five cents. So if you had a buck, you could take your date to the movies, treat her to a coke or a hot chocolate, and get her back to the dorm before curfew at ten o'clock.

◆ Above: *John Whalen and Earl Westervelt (background) in Washington, D.C., for the Fifth North American Wildlife Conference, in March 1940*

◆ Left: *Sometimes the Hillers' trips took them north, even to Canada, where members of the 1938 summer crew went fishing before school started. The trip panned out well for John Whalen and Joe Dell, and Walt Crissey enjoyed the experience too.*

There were several haunts where the price of a big pitcher of beer was fifty cents—Leonardo's on Eddy Street, Jim's on Stewart Avenue, the Pine Tavern, Zinck's, and of course the Dutch Kitchen in the old Ithaca Hotel. The Dutch was famous as a rendezvous for returning alumni, and when things began to roll, the sounds of Cornell songs could be heard out on the street.

One of the favorite beer hall frolics was singing verses of limericks. Each verse ended with: "That was a cute little verse. Sing us another one too." Then another student was pointed at, and he had to continue with another verse—no repeats. The one who failed to come up with a verse had to buy the next pitcher of beer. It was prudent to learn your limericks or stay out of the beer halls.

Mixed parties at fraternities had to be cleared with the university so arrangements could be made for university-approved chaperons. Before Spring Weekend festivities, when it was common for male students to invite out-of-town girlfriends, partitions had to be erected in the fraternity houses to separate male and female lodging areas, and chaperons were always present to see that nobody blew down the walls of Jericho.

I have visited the campus on numerous occasions over the years and have observed the many changes in lifestyles and social habits. My only lament is that I was born fifty years too soon.

And Don Foley adds a few words about Don Spittler:

No partying for me—you had to have $$$ for that. But we had plenty of fun. I lived in the same dorm as Don Spittler, and as you can imagine, he kept the place pretty well livened up. I don't remember whether he was in the "battle of the fire hoses" or not, but I know they had to pump and squeegee the place out. There is probably a story behind the beer barrel he had hung on his wall too.

One thing I was rather proud of then (that makes me weak now) was running all the way up Buffalo Street hill just for the hell of it—or maybe just to quaff a beer at Leonardo's.

LOST: A SEMESTER; FOUND: A CAREER

C. WILLIAM SEVERINGHAUS

*L*IKE MANY STUDENTS, *Bill Severinghaus ran out of money and had to take a semester off. As 1936 drew to a close, Bill's father told him that there were no funds for him to continue college. He was just then finishing the first semester of his junior year. What could he do? He had an idea.*

I knew that Ike Walton had been scheduled to make a deer survey in the Adirondacks, but Ike had just died, and they were looking for someone to take his place. I told Frank Edminster of my situation and that I would like the job if I could do the work. He believed I could do the work. He called Albany and talked to Gardiner Bump and called Elizabethtown and talked to Bob Darrow. He convinced them that my work on the Hill was good and told them he was recommending me for the job.

I went to see Dean Ladd in Roberts Hall, and I told him my story. He called my teachers and learned they had already written the final exams. I could take the five exams on Thursday and Friday, but then I would have to leave Ithaca immediately, so I had no chance to tell anyone the content of the exams. I agreed. I took the exams two weeks before academic instruction was finished.

I had all my good clothes and two pairs of boots in a big leather traveling bag and a big pack basket. Dad's .30-06 rifle was strapped to the leather case, and he had me take his .22-caliber and .38-caliber Smith and Wessons with me in the leather case. Mom and Dad, my brother Jordan, and my sister Mary Ellen took me to the East Ithaca train station, and I took the afternoon milk train to Utica (it stopped a hundred times) and then a train to Albany. Mother had made a big picnic supper for me, which I carried in a bag. I ate supper going to Utica.

I arrived in Albany after midnight. A young man in a strange city. I put my jacket on, I put the pack basket on my back with the straps over my shoulders, and with my big leather case in one hand and a big package in my other hand I walked out onto the sidewalk. To the left a hundred yards or so and across the street was a little lighted sign: "Hotel." I walked down to it and in the door.

At the desk the clerk asked me, "What do you want?" "A room for the night." "A room for the night?" "Yes, a room for just one night." "Oh. Sign here. That's five dollars. Now!" I paid. "Up the stairs, turn left, first door on the right. Here's your key." Up I went. There was a double bed, a washbowl, and running water. I undressed, got into my pajamas, and went to bed.

Just as I was dozing off, there was a knock on the door, and a female voice said: "Mister, open the door. I want to talk to you." I replied, "I'm in bed and want to go to sleep." She talked more and then left. Then another female voice: "Mister, I got something for you. Please open the door so we can talk." More talk by her, and she left. I pondered what that was about, but I soon went to sleep.

Next morning I washed, shaved, packed my bags, and took them downstairs. There was a telephone, so I called Mr. Bump. After a few introductory comments he asked where I was. When I explained, he said: "There's no hotel on that street near the station. All the hotels are up the hill from the next corner on State Street." We talked more about the puzzle of where I was, but I finally suggested that he come to the railroad station and go further to the left, and I would be standing on the sidewalk with my big leather bag and pack basket. He'd be there in thirty minutes. On time he drove up in a Buick four-door with license number 958. He helped load my stuff, and we drove away.

"Do you know where you were last night? That's a whorehouse."

On Monday Mr. Robert Darrow drove down from Elizabethtown, and Mr. Bump introduced me to my new boss. I stayed with Bob and Manda Darrow in Elizabethtown for several days. During that time I read Ben Bradley's journal of his work and observations during the winter of 1935 and numerous reports that had been written about deer in the Adirondacks, winter feeding, overwinter mortality, survey techniques, and how to make and record observations and fill out data sheets. I heard about the Moose River Plains, Gerald Kenwell, and Burt Brown. I would be in the Beaver Lake camp belonging to a Mr. Chapin. Burt Brown was the caretaker and would be my cook and resident companion. I would come out about March 10, and then I would go to another deer-wintering area from March 15 to 31.

Bob asked if there was any place in the Adirondacks that I had been hunting or fishing. Yes, there was. When I was sixteen, Dad had taken me deer hunting at Charley Lawrence's camp on Hayes Brook, which was on the south side of the Debar Mountain Game Refuge. I had also been there fishing.

◆ *The private camp of Mr. Chapin on Beaver Lake, Hamilton County, provided a base for Ben Bradley and Bill Severinghaus during their winter deer surveys on the Moose River Plains in 1935 and 1937. The log construction is native red spruce.*

"Wonderful," Bob exclaimed. "There is a deer yard there. Could you get permission to stay in that camp for two weeks in March?" I called Dad in Ithaca, Dad called Charley, Dad called me, I called Charley, and a deal was made to use the camp.

I was probably the happiest young man in New York. Dad had taken me hunting at Limekiln Lake and Seventh Lake Mountain when I was ten and Debar when I was sixteen, and now I would be making deer surveys for the state in the two places I had previously been with Dad. How lucky can one kid be?

About January 15, 1937, Bob and I were at Gerald and Ina Kenwell's hotel on Sixth Lake, and the next morning Bob and I walked on snowshoes to Beaver Lake. Each of us had a heavy pack, Bob's about seventy pounds and mine more than a hundred pounds. Bob left his pack at Kenwell's halfway camp on the Red River, and we went on to Beaver Lake via Mitchell Ponds and Bob West's camp.

I met Burt Brown. Bob stayed overnight. Next morning I went back to the halfway camp with Bob. He departed, and I returned to Beaver Lake carrying his load of data sheets, and so on, in my pack basket. There I was, ten miles out in the woods, in the center of the Adirondacks' biggest wilderness area, a total stranger, with maps and a compass and a camp caretaker who was a hermit except for a few weeks each summer and fall when men were in camp trout fishing or deer hunting.

That evening Burt showed me where everything was placed. "You hang your outdoor clothes there and your boots over here. That's my chair. The water bucket is here. That's your drinking cup, and this is mine. That's my chair! The stove-lid handle always hangs over the stove on this nail. The wood box is full all the time, so you don't have to go out in bad weather. That's my chair! I don't use the main building in the winter, and there's nothing you need to know about it, but I'll show it to you tomorrow. It and the glass porch are used when Mr. Chapin and all his friends are here. The canned food is on this shelf, the dishes are on these shelves, and that's my chair!" It was terribly obvious that I was to know that only Burt sat in the padded platform rocker by the window.

Burt cooked supper and breakfast every day, and there was plenty to eat, but I made my own lunch with Burt's bread or leftover pancakes. Everything went well with Burt and me.

But in early February we had salt pork for breakfast and supper for about three days. I screwed up my courage and asked Burt about it. He said, "I'm all out of fresh meat." So I said, "Tomorrow I'll go to Inlet and get a basketful to bring back." That I did, but I had to walk to Sixth Lake, because nobody came along to give me a ride from Limekiln to Kenwell's Hotel. Gerald could not understand why we had run out of beef and pork. But we went to the store in Inlet, and he bought enough meat to overflow my big pack basket, and then I had him buy some oatmeal, cornflakes, and shredded wheat for me.

◆ *During a Conservation Department inspection, winter 1935: Burt Brown, caretaker; Vic Skiff, department field agent; Gardiner Bump; Gerald Kenwell, hotel owner and guide; Earl Holm, game farms supervisor; Frank Edminster; and Bob Darrow*

Ina asked me what I would like for supper, and I had two requests, fresh vegetables and a fruit salad. She had both. That night in Inlet there was a community dance. They invited me to go, and Gerald found some slippers I could wear instead of my boots. I soon learned that Geraldine, Kenwell's daughter, was a good dance partner who could follow my lead in any step I took. I had a great time.

Next morning Gerald took me to Limekiln Lake, and I walked back to Beaver via Mitchell Ponds, about ten miles. There was an oilcloth cover over the top of the overfull pack basket, and the packages on top were the cereal. Burt looked at them

and exclaimed, "Chicken feed—I don't eat it!" Breakfast was always sourdough pancakes, maple syrup, and pork sausage.

A week or two later Burt went into town for the weekend. The second night he was gone, there were several *thump, thump, thump*s on the cabin wall that awakened me. I listened, and they were repeated. I could not figure out what they were, so I took Dad's .38 and a flashlight and went outside. Against the cabin wall in a V-shaped two-foot-deep trench under the roof overhang were Burt's tiger cat and a snowshoe rabbit it had caught. The cat was trying to kill it, and the rabbit was kicking with its hind legs. Its feet hit the log cabin wall, *thump, thump, thump*. I had forgotten to call the cat in before I went to bed.

When Burt returned, in the middle of the afternoon, he had a terrible hangover and looked sick. When I came in, he had the fire started in the stove and was preparing supper. I learned later that he had sobered up on the trail with a bottle of gin and a bottle of maple syrup. His recipe: Take one swig of gin, and fill the space in the gin bottle with the maple syrup. Repeat until the maple syrup bottle is empty. Then finish off the content of the gin bottle.

A Field Trip to Moose River Plains

W. MASON LAWRENCE

I remember a field trip to Beaver Lake in the winter of 1937.

We left Fernow Hall about four o'clock on a Friday afternoon. Eddie Edminster was driving, and Paul Christner, Harland Fields, John Morse, and perhaps some others also went. We drove to a camp on Sixth Lake, where we had dinner and stayed overnight.

Saturday morning we left the trailhead at Limekiln Lake for the Moose River Plains and Beaver Lake. There was about ten to twelve inches of snow on the ground. I don't think we used snowshoes.

Three or four hours later we met up with Bill Severinghaus. Bill was on snowshoes and carried a heavy pack basket as if it were a tote bag. We then proceeded the three or so miles to Beaver Lake camp.

During Saturday afternoon and Sunday morning we observed deer-wintering areas and conditions around Beaver Lake and in the Moose River Plains. We observed particularly the experiment in progress of emergency winter feeding. Deer cakes weighing about fifty pounds, made of molasses, soybeans, and so on—devised, I believe, by Dr. McKay of the Cornell nutrition department—were attached to trees at a suitable height for feeding deer. As it turned out, that type of feeding proved costly and ineffective. In fact, it caused more problems than it solved by concentrating deer in limited areas.

On Sunday we hiked back to Limekiln Lake and returned to Ithaca. I believe Bill and the caretaker at Beaver Lake camp came out with us to replenish their supplies. Our hungry crew had put quite a dent in them.

We thoroughly enjoyed the trip. It was a unique winter experience, even for those of us experienced in the outdoors. We also enjoyed good food and fine fellowship. I remember especially an enthusiastic game of hearts on Saturday evening in camp.

One afternoon in late February or early March, I was making a 100 percent survey of the one-mile square at the east end of Beaver Lake. Each north-south line crossed the Beaver Lake trail. On one of my laps, as I came north to the trail, I saw tracks of several people. I walked west about a quarter-mile, and there they were around a fire in the middle of the trail. It was Frank Edminster's wildlife-management class from Cornell! When I left Ithaca, Frank had told me that he would try to bring the class to the Moose River. They were standing around the fire because, having crossed several north-south tracks of mine, Frank was confused about which way to go to Beaver Lake.

We went to camp, and Burt and I started a big fire in the fireplace of the main lodge while the class got warm in our quarters. At least half the class did not have the proper boots and clothes for the trip, and it was good luck that the temperature was just below freezing and sunny. They had carried food, which they unpacked and gave to Burt to cook. They all had bedrolls or sleeping bags and slept on the floor.

That night and the next day I explained to the class my work, record-keeping system, survey techniques, and findings. I went with the class to the Moose River Plains, the hay shed where the deer cakes were stored, a couple of feeding stations, the Sumner River Plains, and the top of Mount Tom, halfway to Red River. I talked to the class about my work and what I knew about a deer-wintering area.

One anecdote from the class visit: Burt had a radio that ran off a six-volt wet cell. He used it only for listening to his programs. One was a serial with a male actor with a strong English accent. In the class there was a graduate student from England with a strong English accent. Burt stood near him whenever he could. (A living, talking English-man was in Burt's camp, and he wasn't missing one minute of watching and listening to him.)

I had many opportunities to practice skills Dad had taught me. All my field surveys were made by compass, and I paced the distances off U.S. Geological Survey maps. I set up a one-mile square east of the Sumner River Plains and closed it within two hundred feet of where I had started. I made two trips around Mount Tom to determine how high the deer were traveling from the winter range. And I had to shoot three fawns in March near Lost Ponds, each with a single shell. (Gerald Kenwell brought them out with his sleigh and team of horses in late March after I had left.) The weight of those fawns would be compared with the weight of fawns dying of starvation.

In early March Burt asked me to help him fill the icehouse. With our snowshoes we packed a smooth runway from the lake to the icehouse. We shoveled snow off a fifty-foot-square patch on the

◆ *Bill and Burt filled the icehouse using the same handmade sled Ben Bradley is using here, in 1935, to distribute deer cakes. The sled was all wood; it didn't even have any nails or screws. Who made it? Bill says Gerald Kenwell; Bob Darrow says Bob Cameron's father, Byron, chief game protector at Saranac Lake in the 1920s.*

lake. The ice blocks were cut with a handsaw and pulled out of the water with ice tongs. We would place two blocks on a sled that Gerald Kenwell had made by hand and pull it up to the icehouse. In two days the icehouse was filled.

About March 15 I packed all I had, said so long to Burt, his yellow tiger tomcat, Matilda, the big red doe, buck, and fawn, and a half a dozen other deer that fed on the soya bean–molasses cakes at Beaver. I left an old pair of slippers and torn rubber boots, shouldered my pack, and headed for Limekiln Lake. At the end of the lake, and about

two hundred feet up the trail, I stopped at an old log on the west side of the trail, and from under it I picked up a pint of apricot brandy. Dad had given it to me when I left home, saying it was for medicinal purposes, and I should hide it near camp; otherwise someone might drink it. When I got to the road at Limekiln, there was no ride (I was out early), so I walked to Kenwell's Hotel on Sixth Lake. I made the fifteen miles in less than three hours. Gerald had not expected me so early.

Bob and Manda Darrow came from Elizabethtown that evening and stayed at Kenwell's. They brought me a check for $100, the most money I had ever seen in one lump.

On March 16 Bob and Manda drove me and Francis LaRue from Inlet in Hamilton County to McColloms in Franklin County. Gurley, as LaRue was known, was a jack-of-all-trades who worked for Gerald. He wanted to go with me to Charley Lawrence's camp (no pay), and Bob approved. We were deposited on March 16 at about ten o'clock in the morning at the trail head, and Bob headed back to Elizabethtown.

It was five miles back to the camp. We had all our food for fourteen days and other personal necessities, data sheets, and so on, on our backs—more than a hundred pounds for each of us. Dad had taught me to use a tumpline across my forehead. I had used it in the Moose River Plains carrying deer cakes, and it was useful now with such heavy packs. We had to walk side by side on our snowshoes, instead of one following in the other's tracks, because we were sinking eight inches in fresh snow, and our stride length was so different. When I counted 100 steps, Gurley counted 130.

We got to the big, burnt white pine in the beaver meadow, where the trail turned west to the camp, half a mile away, but I could not find the trail, covered as it was with three feet of snow. I left Gurley at the meadow and with the compass made a trip of more than half a mile due west, turned a loop, and came back out. No camp. I made another loop. No camp.

So we went into a balsam stand, built a lean-to of boughs, and started cutting firewood. (Dad had told me to take my hatchet with me when traveling.) We had bread and meat cooked over our open fire for supper, and we had our shelter. We cut several tamarack trees and dragged them to the fire. We had a pile of boughs to sit on. We would heat our front and sides and then turn our

◆ **Above:** *Frank Edminster in November 1936 crossing the south branch of the Moose River on a cable maintained by Gerald Kenwell for use by hunters going to his camp on Otter Brook*

◆ **Right:** *Bill Severinghaus on March 16, 1937, beside Route 30 just below Meacham Lake, where Bob and Manda Darrow left him and Francis LaRue to snowshoe in to Bill's uncle's camp south of Debar Mountain*

backs to the fire, rest our heads on our knees, and get some sleep.

In an hour and a quarter we would awake because of chill, rebuild the fire, and cut more trees. We burned fourteen five-inch trees that night. Next morning on the first trip back toward camp by compass I found it. I had missed it the previous day by about a hundred yards. The key was over the door, and I was inside. I went back for Gurley and the packs, and we were in camp by 7:00 a.m. Soon we had a fire in the cookstove,

hot coffee in our cups, and pancakes and sausage for breakfast on the table. It was the first night in the woods for both of us, and we had done well.

I was enjoying the trip, because I had seen the area first while deer hunting with Dad in 1932 and again while trout fishing in May or June 1934. While deer hunting, our drives always started at the wire that surrounded the Debar Mountain Game Refuge and went south. Now my work took me inside the refuge, into forbidden land. I found the caretaker's camp, which I had not known existed.

One day on the meadow when I was coming back to camp, I met a beaver trapper skinning a beaver. I stopped and talked. He walked in every other day. I invited him to stay with us. He agreed that he would on his next trip. He gave me the beaver carcass, and I went to camp. That night I stuffed the beaver with a bread dressing and roasted it in the oven, as I had seen Mother do with a raccoon. It was delicious. A layer of gravy formed when it cooled that was a tasty filling for a sandwich.

About March 30 Bob Darrow drove to the trail head, and Gurley and I walked out of the camp and met him. Then we went to Inlet and stayed overnight. Next morning I picked up what I had left at Kenwell's, we said our good-byes and thanked the Kenwells, and Bob and I headed for Elizabethtown. He talked to me about my fieldwork and my data sheets for a couple of days, and then he drove me to Albany. I was given two more paychecks, each $100, and I was elated. So much money!

We talked with Gardiner Bump for a couple of days, because he was interested in the results of the deer feeding—how much they ate and whether a way had been found to allow fawns to eat but not adult deer. I had designed and built several racks. But the adults would not let fawns eat when they could not eat. That dominance was true of both bucks and does. Before they would let the fawns eat, we had to open several cans, one for each adult and one or two extra for the fawns. Bob and I stayed at the Bumps' house.

I gave Bump the crop and gizzard contents of several grouse I had collected in the Moose River Plains. He had asked me to kill the grouse when all vegetation was covered with ice or frozen snow, to learn what they ate under those conditions. I had shot them with Dad's .22 revolver when I found them sitting in the trees.

Bump had work for me to do from April through August. Surveying quail-liberation sites to determine survival, if any, during April and May and collecting grouse and some other game species for disease studies from June through August. The pay was $100 a month and board, room, and travel expenses. Whoopee!

I went from Albany to Ithaca by train. The family was happy to see me, and I returned to Dad the pint bottle of apricot brandy, reporting that I had had no medicinal use for it. Dad was pleased. He opened the bottle, and we all had a drink in celebration of my return.

I took several bird skins to Dr. Sutton (three-toed woodpeckers and Canada jays) and some shrew skins to Dr. Hamilton. They had asked me to collect them.

On September 1 I was home. But there were twenty days before school would start. While I was in Delaware County, I had seen a sign at a farmhouse: "Farm Help Wanted." I told Mother and Dad, and they drove me to Charley DeGolyer's farm near Delhi. He would hire me for a dollar a day, my board, and my room. I asked what the other men got. Two dollars a day, board, and room. I made him a deal: If he'd put me against his best man, and I could keep even with him at all fieldwork, he'd pay me two dollars a day. He agreed. I told Dad and Mother, and they drove off.

We cut corn by hand with a corn knife. The guy I worked against was certain he could best a col-lege kid. I had fun staying even with him most of the day and keeping just ahead of him late in the day. For me it was a fun contest. For him it was difficult, because the other hands kidded him about the kid keeping up with him all day.

Late one afternoon Charley wanted a cow brought down from the upper farm. We drove up in a car. The cow was caught and haltered, and they left me to walk it back to the lower farm, a couple of miles away. While on Tom Newton's farm at Sheldrake, I had seen cattle buyers put a cow into the back of a truck by twisting its tail. So I gave the cow the full length of the rope, grabbed its tail, and twisted. It moved away from the pain. We ran, and we ran, and we ran. In twenty minutes we came into the driveway. Holding the rope, I went up to the kitchen window and announced my presence. The men came out. There were strange looks on all faces. The cow was put in the barn. I washed up and sat down at the dinner table. It was rather quiet. I asked, "Is there something wrong?" There sure was. The cow was a setup. It was expected I would be hours pulling that cow to the lower farm and would be late for supper.

September 20 came, and Dad and Mother came to get me. Charley DeGolyer paid me $40 and wished me a good year in college. Soon I was back with the family in Ithaca, ready to enroll for the fall semester and looking forward to more experiences on Connecticut Hill.

Anna Allen Wright and Albert Hazen Wright on a coast-to-coast trip in summer 1925 to obtain information and take photographs for their classic Handbook of Frogs and Toads. *This stop was in El Paso, Texas.*

CHAPTER NINE

Those Great Professors

MENTORS AND FRIENDS
WITH A
LASTING INFLUENCE

AMONG OUR DIVERSE UNIVERSITIES *a few, by general agreement, are far above standard academic institutions. In a word, they are great. But what is greatness? What makes it? How is it conferred? Does greatness arise out of unusually productive laboratories? Do great thinkers make great universities? Does it come from a steady stream of scholarly papers in the academic journals? Or is it great professors?*

After all, it is the professors who bind together the many pieces that constitute a university. If students believe their professors are great, then the university is great. Cornell's Hillers insist their professors were great. The passage of five or six decades has not dimmed the warm memories they have of their great professors, as the quotations that follow testify. According to Earl Westervelt, "The stalwarts of the teaching staff at Cornell really got through to us, and what we learned from them went with us to our varied assignments after graduation."

When we asked the Hillers which professors were still fresh in their memories, the name Arthur A. Allen was mentioned again and again.

Dr. Allen was Don Spittler's faculty advisor, and he vividly recalls his first consultation with the professor:

Initially apprehensive, as a freshman would be, I soon lost my anxiety in an atmosphere of congeniality. He invited me to take a seat, and his first question was: "So you come from Lake View. Where is that? Is it near Hamburg?" I responded with a surprised "Yes!" He then asked me if I knew of Bill Allen, the Town of Hamburg supervisor. Again surprised, I replied, "Yes, and my father knows him well." Dr. Allen replied, "He's my brother." From that point I relaxed to enjoy his kind words of advice. As I left his office, I realized that I had met not only a kind mentor but also a friend.

◆ A. A. Allen raised these ruffed grouse from captive adults. His work, hailed as the achievement that followed two centuries of futile efforts, is at the root of attempts to save endangered species, such as the peregrine falcon, by hand-rearing methods.

Don Foley has equally warm memories: "I can mention Doc Allen only with the greatest respect. He was always cool and calm, even in times of great stress. Maybe that's why he was so famous and world-honored. Yet no detail was too small for his at-tention, and his door was always open. He was advisor to most of us 'problematic' wildlifers."

Herbert Schrauer remembers his enthusiasm: "Dr. A. A. Allen was my advisor, and I took all his courses. A great, enthusiastic teacher. All the great teachers in the biological field—Bill Hamilton and the rest—were great influences. My memory gets hazy, but one professor's opening remark remains: 'I don't mind your falling asleep, but don't snore and wake up your neighbors.'"

Chuck Mason reflects: "A. A. Allen was my faculty advisor, but more importantly, he guided my transition from the Reed bird books to the birds of the world. And to a lifetime of greater understanding and appreciation, both of birds and of photography." Chuck was bird watching in the pre-Peterson era, when Chester Reed's Bird Guide was the only simple illustrated guide to our common birds. Dr. Allen took Chuck from merely looking at birds to the larger dimension of serious bird study.

Professor Allen influenced Royce Brower's career direction:

A. A. Allen really stands out in my recollections of ornithology. He was a big part in my moving to work as a biologist with the Soil Conservation Service. Even though they didn't need me as a biologist for long, it did get me into work in the conservation field, and I never could forget that portion of agriculture. (Oh, yes. I did get wildlife consideration into lots of farm conservation plans.)

It was not unusual for Dr. Allen to have a memorable impact on people and events. One of those many people is Earl Westervelt:

Having grown up in Ithaca, I was first introduced to the ruffed grouse survey as a teenager through acquaintance with Dr. Arthur A. Allen. He was offering five dollars to anyone who would show him a grouse nest containing eggs. He wanted to hatch them as part of a propagation project of the NYS Conservation Department.

I had found a nest while hiking with Boy Scout Troop No. 6 in Watkins Glen and called Dr. Allen. He picked me up at my home in his new 1931 Buick touring car. We located the nest, but it had been broken up by a raccoon. He took the shells for further examination. I was disappointed, but the fifty cents he gave me was the start of a friendship that was to last throughout my high school and college careers. He was my faculty advisor during my four years at Cornell.

Professor Allen's May and December all-day bird counts were legendary. Bill Severinghaus comments on a Christmas count in which he participated:

Each group of three or four was assigned a location for the count. We were there before dawn and conscientiously covered our area and identified and counted what we saw. Late in the afternoon we all gathered at Dr. Allen's home. There we sat on the floor, and Dr. and Mrs. Allen walked among us with sandwiches and hot chocolate. Dr. Allen asked questions of each of us: "Where were you? What birds did you see? How many did you see? Was the wind cold?" I believe he spoke to everyone. What I remember is that I was recognized. Then each of the leaders reported the species and number seen, and a total was made and compared with previous years.

◆ Left: *It's only 6:00 a.m., but bird-watchers have come from miles around to join A. A. Allen in search of spring migrants.* Above: *A well-hidden Dr. Allen prepares to take a photograph. He used slides and films in public lectures all over the country to awaken an interest in birds and bird preservation.*

Not only was Professor Allen a friendly, caring individual. He wrote a doctoral dissertation on the red-winged blackbird that provided a new model for studying birds ecologically. The Book of Bird Life, the first college text on the subject, went through eleven printings. His skill in combining photography with writing and lecturing earned him the praise and adulation of professional and amateur bird students worldwide. At meetings of the American

The Go-away-ster

ALBERT G. HALL

Dr. Allen was my advisor and a great professor. Very serious. I remember he wanted a woodcock nest for a picture. It so happened that I found one on Connecticut Hill. I told Crissey, who told me to talk to Dr. Allen about it. I did and made a date to meet him on the Hill. Great. I was completely absorbed in watching his procedure, but he needed no help. He just thanked me and said calmly, "You can go now."

What I didn't know at the time was that Professor Allen was expressing more than appreciation. He was using me as a "go-away-ster." After he got his blind, camera, and flash lamps set up, Doc almost always had a person walk away so that the bird would think everyone was gone and would therefore return to its nest sooner.

Ornithologists' Union in the 1940s and 1950s, 40 percent of the scientific papers were presented by his graduates. Professor Allen's innumerable contributions to ornithology as well as to people are memorialized in the institution he founded: Cornell's Laboratory of Ornithology.

Fred Garrett comments, "Lovable A. A. Allen presided without apparent effort over the budding American hobby of bird study." And he wonders, "Was he just lucky, or did he foresee that this out-of-the-mainline academic field would make him one of the best-known members of the Cornell faculty?"

Remembered in a different context, but no less respected and admired, was the noted mammalogist William J. Hamilton, Jr. Professor Hamilton was basically a shy person who concealed his shyness behind a mask of tall tales and startling behavior. The mask was so well contrived that few penetrated it. But those who did were richly rewarded. His credentials? He was an authority on mammalian ecology, populations, distribution, and food habits, the author of two basic books on mammalogy and 225 scientific publications, and a president of the Ecological Society of America. And he was one of Albert Hazen Wright's last doctoral students.

Don Foley seems to have penetrated the Hamilton mask:

Bill Hamilton was one of a kind. When they made him, they threw the mold away.

We all appreciated his light-hearted and even comical approach, but underneath he was dead serious that the lesson be learned. I never got to play poker in his company, but he must have been a whiz. His poker face could fool the most astute.

On one field trip to the university orchards we were to collect as many meadow voles as we could. It was for one of his many mammalian researches. There were ten or twelve students catching and tossing mice to Dr. Hamilton, who caught 'em and dropped 'em into a pack basket. The mice were all supposed to be dead, but I'm afraid I flipped a live one to Bill. Well, it promptly bit him on the finger, and we all heard his bellow, but the mice were coming at him so fast, he never knew which one of us did it.

Royce Brower did well in his favorite professor's course: "Just before the final in his mammalogy course, Professor Hamilton offered to bet that no one would get a perfect grade. Well, John Morse got 99, and there was one score of 100. I done it! He was probably the professor I enjoyed most."

Professor Hamilton's famous tall stories regularly progressed from the false but believable to the patently ridiculous, to which the auditor was eventually forced to react. Don Spittler provides an example:

During a Zoology 8 lecture Bill was discussing the Carchariidae (the true sharks), and he told of a large gray specimen that was landed off Long Island. When they brought the catch to shore, it caused great concern, and they decided to eviscerate the beast. Much to their horror, they found the remains of a human. Positive identification was impossible, but they concluded that the victim was a navy man.

After a slight pause one of the students in the front row took the bait and asked, "How did they know that?" With a poker face Doc replied, "He was tattooed on both arms." Bursts of sporadic laughter filled the room, but as always, there were those who

E. MAKOWSKI

◆ *These lucky students are visiting the Connecticut Hill beaver swamp with the noted mammalogist, and famous teller of tall tales, Prof. William J. Hamilton, Jr.*

CORNELIUS W. KUHN

Professor Hamilton taught at a time when biologists placed great emphasis on acquiring intimate knowledge of the organism in its natural environment. Accordingly, extensive fieldwork was a feature of their courses, and they—not teaching assistants—led the field trips.

I remember the time we all went on a field trip to Michigan Hollow. Don Spittler was my partner as we walked and observed across the ice of a beaver pond. Suddenly we both went through the ice into water up to our chins. We made it to solid earth, and Dr. Hamilton put us to trotting up and down the road while he finished the summary lecture for the rest. We ended up healthy after drying off at school.

failed to grasp Doc's punch line. The confused look on their faces indicated their bewilderment. Obviously they were not aware that the trademark of a seasoned salt at that time was a string of tattoos up and down his arms.

Eugene Gerberg contributes this vintage Hamilton tall story: "I believe this occurred on one of Hamilton's field trips. The class was in the woods, snow was on the ground, and Hamilton pointed out rabbit tracks. One of the students asked if they were recent tracks. Hamilton answered, 'Sure, feel them. They're still warm.'"

Chuck Mason knew what Professor Hamilton was up to: "The rather pedantic tone, delivered with a trace of Big City accent and punctuated by an occasional slide, kept you scribbling madly, trying to catch up. Then the zinger—which you also started to record before doing a double take on the preposterous tag line. But it sure kept you awake."

Bill Severinghaus sums it up:

He gave a short lecture at the beginning of each lab session, and at the end of the lecture he would tell us what the assigned reading for the lecture was.

Those Great Professors

When he returned our first test papers, a student said, "Dr. Hamilton, I have here in my notes exactly what you said in your lecture, and that's the answer I wrote on the exam." Hamilton said, "At the end of every lecture I give you the assigned reading for that lecture." After that class I was talking to Art Cook, a fellow Connecticut Hiller, and we came to realize that we should remember all the assigned reading but that we could never be certain what we should remember of his lecture.

One afternoon at the beginning of the lab Dr. Hamilton began with a story about a pocket gopher that escaped from its cage, ran over to the open window, and fell to its death. At the end of the lab he asked, "What did you learn from the pocket gopher's death?" There were a couple of comments, and then he remarked: "You must learn to interpret what you see and hear. The prairies of the Midwest are flat. The gopher has no perception of height. Therefore, it thought the ground was on the same level as the window ledge."

On a field trip to Spencer marsh some of us were walking behind Dr. Hamilton as he told us what to do when we entered the marsh. A few students were flanking him. A girl was a few steps to his right. All of a sudden she sank in the water over her head. When she came up, someone pulled her out, and she regained her footing. Dr. Hamilton turned to the class saying, "When we entered the marsh, I told you to follow behind me." After that we did.

Another oft-mentioned great professor was the celebrated zoologist Albert Hazen Wright. "A scientist of the old school" is Nick Drahos's characterization. An early interest in plants stayed with A. H. Wright through his junior year at Cornell, when he changed his major to zoology, focusing on the cold-blooded vertebrates. He and his wife, Anna (Professor Allen's sister), spent summers observing and photographing every fish, amphibian, and reptile they could find, amassing a file of twelve thousand negatives. Together they wrote definitive works on frogs, toads, and snakes.

Most Hillers knew Professor Wright through his full-year course, Zoology 8. W. J. Hamilton was at one time his teaching assistant. Dr. Wright was clearly another of those great professors, as Don Foley observes: "Albert Hazen Wright was a zoologist's zoologist. Even though he was in his 'golden years' when I was exposed to him, he hadn't lost any zip. He could relate zoological (and other) discoveries worldwide—because he had been there. He seemed to have a special liking for the prince of Monaco. And the habitat of the purple salamander."

Nick Drahos held Professor Wright in especially high esteem:

Doc Wright probably had the most amazing zoological memory of all time. He could spout scientific names and life histories of fishes (fresh and ocean), mammals, birds, frogs, and snakes with abandon. His tales of former associates like David Starr Jordan were fascinating. I wish that portable tape recorders had been invented at that time. What a gold mine of lore he was! His Prohibition stories entertained us immensely. Fuzzy Hamilton (he was nearly bald) told a few whoppers, but he couldn't hold a candle to Wright, even when he was telling a true story.

Dr. Wright was noted for digressing frequently in his lectures, as Don Spittler vividly recalls:

The Zoology 8 class was seated in the dingy classroom in the loft of McGraw Hall, waiting for Dr. Wright to arrive. Bill Hamilton paced up and down the left side of the room, and he muttered one of his usual witty remarks that prompted an outburst of laughter from those who heard him. At that point Dr. Wright entered, greeted the class in a cheerful manner, and began to search through his vest pockets. Finding nothing, he looked up somewhat confused and said, "Guess I forgot my notes, so this morning we will have the usual hodgepodge." Whereupon he started to talk about the trip he and Mrs. Wright had taken in their Model T Ford to the wilds of the Okefenokee Swamp in Georgia. Some event in the journey triggered another thought, and he compared it to a situation in his hometown of Webster, New York. And so it went.

Professor Wright remains very much alive in Chuck Mason's memory:

A. H. Wright was almost a stereotype of the older college professor of the late 1930s. While he and Anna were tolerant of the teaching load of the semesters, they lived for the summer fieldwork with their beloved frogs and toads.

My most vivid memories of AHW are of his almost sprinting up and down the aisles of the lecture hall, pointing to a small picture in an aged tome he carried, to illustrate his talk on some extinct deep-sea fish or reptile.

His lecture notes were also in character. The yellowed sheets were fragile and dog-eared and had not been updated for years. But there was little need to update the sections on extinct critters until discoveries were made in future decades.

Don Spittler informs us that Dr. Wright loved baseball:

As a youth, he played with the local nine, usually on Sundays, in his hometown of Webster, New York. Such activity on the Sabbath riled the preacher of the church his family attended, and he proclaimed that those who participated were having a rendezvous with Satan. Doc's parents agreed. Now what was poor Albert to do? He could not bear to tell his teammates that he would no longer play on Sundays, so he hid his uniform

◆ *Albert Hazen Wright, the celebrated vertebrate zoologist, on a herpetology-class field trip near Ithaca, probably in 1933*

in the barn. After the Sunday meal, under the pretense of tending the livestock and taking a stroll, he would grab his uniform and take off across the back field to the ball diamond in Webster. The scheme worked for a while, but word got back to the Wrights that Albert had been seen playing baseball on Sunday. The chastisement he received remained a sore spot in his life.

Doc used to ask, "If the Lord is so omnipotent, why did He let the devil get all the good games on his side?"

Prof. Bristow Adams was a man of diverse talents, interests, and accomplishments. As a trained artist, he provided the Bering Fur Seal Commission with illustrations of living seals made in the Pribilof Islands. His urge to write, edit, and organize found expression in establishing several literary publications, including Pathfinder *magazine. A stint with the U.S. Forest Service, in charge of the office of information, prepared him well for employment at Cornell, where he assumed responsibility for the format and editorial quality of extension and experiment station publications. Professor Adams established several journalism courses and taught a course called Conservation of Natural Resources. How did the Hillers regard him? Al Hall provides a capsule summary:*

B.A. was a wonderful person and a great professor. As I remember, every Monday night he had an open house where you could discuss anything or enjoy yourself at checkers, chess, or bridge. I chose chess and remember playing John Whalen one night. After three hours we quit with no winner. Coffee, tea, punch, and cookies were always there. And who can forget the gentleman at Barton Hall Heptagonal track meets—the man with top hat and tails? In my freshman year his course Conservation of Natural Resources began with the three *exes*: "exploration, exploitation, and exhaustion." What better way to launch such a course for freshmen? He hit you between the eyes, and of course it still applies.

After six decades Don Foley remembers: "Bristow Adams had not only a wry sense of humor but also a keen and complete knowledge of his subject. He caught a lot of know-it-alls off base in his time. I especially valued his open houses every Monday night, when he'd have a crowd of students at his home."

Chuck Mason was another Bristow Adams fan. He recalls:

At the first session of Bristow Adams's course on conservation of natural resources he gazed out over the rows—many were football players and hotel students—and sternly delivered a warning: "Some of you may have heard that this is a snap course, but let me assure you—it is!"

A snap it may have been, but also interesting and thought-provoking. Topics ranged from saving the fur seals to the young men of the world already at war—"They are natural resources too, you know."

Bill Severinghaus remembers the seminar meetings led by Professor Adams on the top floor of Fernow Hall, in front of the fireplace:

◆ *Former students of one of Cornell's great professors—Bristow Adams—still hold warm memories of his open houses on Monday evenings.*

He was retired from full-time teaching, but at those seminars he talked about the history of forestry, the pioneers of the forestry movement, the state and federal forest service, the history and value of our national parks and forests, and his general philosophy of conservation. Of course we also discussed the wise use of natural resources and the difference between preservation and conservation.

Don Spittler comments on the professor's impeccable attire:

Then there was Mr. Esquire, properly known as Prof. Bristow Adams. He wore the latest in men's fashions, displaying exquisite taste that befitted his posture. As he strolled into the classroom, his appearance commanded immediate attention. His manner was as suave as his appearance, and his broad knowledge of the subject and his ability to impart it to the class were most impressive.

Prof. George C. Embody could spark interest in fishes, even though they do not usually excite vertebrate-zoology students. He began his distinguished career in the physical sciences. Cornell-trained like Allen, Hamilton, and Wright, he researched birds, crustacea, the life history of fishes, fish diseases and nutrition, and the problems of game fish production—a field in which he was preeminent. His formulation of a standard stocking policy, widely adopted in the United States and Canada, earned him lasting fame.

To Mason Lawrence, Professor Embody was a giant:

The three giants of the 1930s in vertebrate zoology were Allen, Embody, and Wright. I knew all three quite well. Allen was a polished, well-organized, and effective lecturer. Wright had a wealth of information and experience and broad interests extending beyond zoology. He was a good and interesting lecturer, but one couldn't predict what any particular lecture would be on or where it would lead. Embody, in my opinion, was the poorest lecturer of the three but the best student of zoology. He was well versed in many fields.

Although the Hillers' interests leaned heavily toward the zoological sciences and the professors who taught them, professors in the botanical fields had their admiring followers also. Don Foley remembers three of them:

W. C. Muenscher, K. M. Wiegand, and Harlan Banks labored unceasingly to make one learn and enjoy the plant world as much as they did. An untiring field man and a real stickler for details, Muenscher was an expert in several aspects of botany. As a student, I appreciated him greatly. I appreciated him even more later, when I was trying to evaluate aquatic habitats as a waterfowl man for the DEC.

Dr. Muenscher, who joined the department of botany in its early years, wrote definitive works on aquatic plants, poisonous plants, and weeds. Dr. Wiegand was the first head of the College of Agriculture's new botany department, and it flourished under his wise leadership. He was regarded as one of the world's leading plant taxonomists. Dr. Harlan Banks, later head of the department, continued the

department's research thrust in the origin of plants while he taught courses in introductory botany.

One gets the impression that Dick Reynolds was so enthralled by his instructors that he thought all of them were great:

It was awesome to attend a lecture where a flamboyant professor like Bristow Adams expounded on the ills of nature, how conservation was needed, and how suggested remedies were over half a life span in coming. I was amazed to learn from Prof. A. A. Allen that there were many hundreds of species of birds that could be identified by their color, posture, flight, and even song. I was astonished by Prof. H. O. Buckman's description of Ithaca's Dunkirk silty clay loam (a viscous, gelatinous, colloidal material). Dr. Charles "Spike" Hayden's lectures in the vet college were as close as I ever came to being exposed to sex education. World-renowned animal nutritionist F. B. Morrison acquainted students with the overwhelming statistics regarding the nutritional value of feeds. Professor Petry's graphic and detailed coverage of plants and their structure made botany enjoyable, while in agricultural economics Prof. Stan Warren explained how the Connecticut Hill area had changed from virgin forest to what was marginal farmland—marginal because of its poor soil and topography. In zoology Dr. A. H. Wright and Dr. W. J. Hamilton were so well versed in the vertebrates that they could tell you an owl's diet by examining the regurgitated pellet.

As the following remembrance by Bill Severinghaus suggests, E. Laurence Palmer was unusual; he was a generalist:

One summer I took a field natural history course taught by Dr. Palmer. His knowledge was impressive. He identified everything: plant, animal, bird, fish, bug, rock, soil, cloud, weather, flower, fungus. But what was most impressive was that with the identity of each item, he explained the ecological relationship of that item to its location and the other conditions of that habitat. A plant was not just a name; it was one small part of a community, and he would explain how the many parts fit together. A mouse, a butterfly, a frog, a rabbit—each was part of a larger habitat, and understanding the intricacies of the habitat was essential to life and progress. His instruction that summer made me realize that nothing in nature is isolated.

With nature and conservation education his fields of teaching and writing, Dr. Palmer had to be a generalist. Preferring to teach outdoors, he challenged his many students to examine carefully, to seek reasons, and to question authority. His Fieldbook of Natural History *is a classic reference.*

Dr. Peter Paul Kellogg, professor of ornithology and bioacoustics, was best known for his work in recording and analyzing birdsongs and other natural sounds. He devoted much effort to developing better equipment for recording in the field. It was Professor Kellogg who, with a student, developed the parabolic reflector so essential to reaching out to distant bird sounds. His interest in producing phonograph recordings of birdsongs led to the publication of a series of discs that not only added to Cornell's reputation in ornithology but also provided much-needed income to the Laboratory of Ornithology. Dr. Kellogg started Cornell's Library of Natural Sounds, a library that continues to grow. Don Spittler shares this memory:

Dr. Allen's able assistant in the ornithology course was Paul Kellogg, who gave several of the lectures. One of his discourses was on birdsongs, and he gave us his rendition of several by whistling the melody. With each rendition he juggled a piece of chalk from hand to hand and pranced about the podium. Undoubtedly the prancing and juggling were subconscious behaviors, but the whole act was quite amusing to me, and I responded with a laugh. He stared at me in an uncomplimentary manner, and from that time on I sensed that I was not one of his favorite students.

The following year I took Dr. Kellogg's course in bird photography. One facet of the course was preparing a ten-minute talk on any aspect of bird life,

R. B. FISCHER

◆ *Trained as an electrical engineer as well as an ornithologist, Dr. Peter Paul Kellogg pioneered in bird-sound recording. It was he who popularized the use of a parabolic reflector to amplify a distant birdsong for the recorder's microphone.*

to be presented on the Cornell radio station. Preparation included a rehearsal with Dr. Kellogg. After my bout in his office he said that the subject matter was fine, but my enunciation needed refinement. He also suggested that I make a serious effort to improve my diction. I appreciated his comments, since I was not conscious of the fact. Now we were even, since we were both guilty of a subconscious trait.

Walt Crissey speaks warmly of a professor of statistics, and with good reason:

Prof. Charles Mottley influenced my life in a major way. It occurred after graduation, while I was trying to make sense out of the mass of grouse survey field data that had been collected over the years. Use of statistical methods for analyzing wildlife data was practically unheard of at the time. Mottley was in the process of adapting statistical techniques for the analysis of fisheries research data. I became acquainted with him through one of his students who was working on the grouse survey.

Chuck had an amazing ability to get people to recognize, with a few pointed questions, the basic problem they were trying to solve, which sometimes was quite different from their original concept. As a reference, he recommended the book *Statistical Methods,* by George Snedecor, and it became my bible. Mottley's assistance and encouragement had more influence on my research ability in subsequent years than any other individual—for which I am eternally grateful.

Contacts with those great professors did not end with graduation. Relationships had been established and nurtured, relationships that went beyond that of professor and student and became lifetime friendships. Here Dick Reynolds recounts an incident that occurred twenty-five years after graduation:

One summer day after unloading a load of pheasant litter (highly valued for its fertility and mulching qualities) at Bill Hamilton's beautiful garden in Cayuga Heights, he presented me with some of his special iris plants. The understanding was that they were to be planted at the Ithaca game farm, in a spot to be designated by my wife, Lois.

We all went to the game farm, and Lois selected the location. Bill dug the first hole, and as the soil fell from the shovel, a five-inch-long night crawler appeared. Before you could say Jack Robinson, Bill seized the worm, stripped away the clinging earth, and devoured it! Needless to say, Lois retreated to her domestic domain, not favorably impressed with his nauseating behavior. The planting continued, and we enjoyed the flowers and Bill for years.

Professor Hamilton's good influence extended even to his students' children. This from Art Hawkins:

Bill and I kept in touch until he passed away in 1989. A postcard came while I was in the hospital having a hip replaced. In it Bill hinted that this would be the last time I would hear from him, and it was. Bill was particularly interested in the observations of my daughter, who lives beside the Superior National Forest in northern Minnesota and works for the U.S. Forest Service in the Boundary

Waters Canoe Area. He encouraged her to write up her observations on wolves, red foxes, and other animals that live nearby. She followed his advice, and a wolf article that appeared in *Audubon* magazine in 1988 and has been reprinted elsewhere is one such story.

In 1925 Dr. Loren Petry joined the faculty at Cornell, where he distinguished himself as an unusually effective administrator and teacher of introductory botany. About twelve thousand students took his course during his thirty-year tenure. Among his other interests was motorless flying, or gliding. Jim Otis says, "I'll never forget watching Dr. Petry tow his daughter Ruth and her glider for a takeoff at the Ithaca airport." He also shares this memory: "Several years after I graduated from Cornell, I had some official work on Cape Cod. I called on Prof. Loren Petry, former head of the botany department, at his retirement home. We had a great visit. I was amazed at his systematic file of slides."

Don Spittler delivers this tribute about the Cornell professors:

In the midfifties I was deeply involved with the small-marsh development program sponsored by the New York State Conservation Department. I was directed to go to the Laboratory of Ornithology at Sapsucker Woods to repair the dike of the manmade marsh. With a backhoe and operator loaned by Dick Reynolds, foreman of the Ithaca game farm, a deep trench was excavated the full length of

the dike. I was at the bottom, knee-deep in mire, when I heard someone say, "How are you making out, Spittler?" I looked up, and stooped over the trench was Dr. Allen. I was amazed that after so many years my former mentor would recognize me and call me by name. Where else except at Cornell would such a bond prevail between students and faculty members?

We Hillers were fortunate. In our days at Cornell we received firsthand instruction from the giants in the fields of natural science: Albert Hazen Wright, Arthur A. Allen, William J. Hamilton, W. C. Muenscher, Bristow Adams, E. L. Palmer, Stan Warren, George Embody, Loren Petry, Arthur Recknagel, and Karl Wiegand, to name a few. Not only did those men prepare the curricula, but they gave the lectures, and they conducted most of the field trips. The close association gave us an exceptional opportunity to know them personally, to share directly in their vast knowledge, and to seek their guidance.

◆

The whole earth is the tomb of heroic men and their story is not graven only in stone over their clay, but abides everywhere, without visible symbol, woven into the stuff of other men's lives.
◆ THUCYDIDES ◆

Asa Smith, Ben Bradley, Gardiner Bump, Janet Bump, and Walt Crissey, all significant pioneers in wildlife management and research in New York State, toured Connecticut Hill when the Hillers returned to Cornell for a reunion in 1982.

CHAPTER TEN

From the Ground Up

THE FIELD OF
WILDLIFE MANAGEMENT
EMERGES

T HE DISCIPLINE OF GAME MANAGEMENT *was just emerging in the decade of the 1930s. Many of the Hillers did not hear of the field until they matriculated in the College of Agriculture at Cornell. What were their perceptions of the new field? To Mason Lawrence the 1930s were "exciting years in the natural resource field, especially in fish and game management."*

Mason continues:

New courses at Cornell, Wisconsin, Michigan, Minnesota, and other major universities; the publication of Leopold's book *Game Management;* the research of Errington, Stoddard, Hazzard, and others; state game and biological surveys; federal programs such as the Civilian Conservation Corps and projects that resulted from the Pittman-Robertson Wildlife Restoration Act—all contributed to the excitement of those times.

Incidentally, Cornell had a course in fish management a couple of years before the game-management course. It met at noon once a week, mostly with guest lecturers, such as Bill Adams, John Greeley, Emmeline Moore, and people prominent in fish culture.

All those activities persuaded me that resource conservation was a challenging and developing field and resulted in my spending a lifetime in it, which I have never regretted.

Don Foley terms them "great times":

We knew we were in on the ground floor of a scientific awakening, and we realized we were being groomed by some of the best minds in the world. For a brief moment, around graduation time, we thought we knew it all. We could go out, get high-paying jobs, and in a few years solve all of wildlife's ills. Little did we know that just around the corner

(in late 1941, anyway) lay a world conflagration that would dash our pretty dreams for many years. In fact, WWII changed everything. When we came back (most of us), it just wasn't the same.

And relating his survey days on the Hill to that same broad context, Ben Bradley writes, "Those were heady days—the birth of modern game management. No stone was left unturned in probing for facts."

"Heady days," "exciting years," "great times," but all amid the Great Depression, whose extensive impacts were made even worse by a vast and prolonged natural disaster, the great drought. Those were our Dust Bowl years; the human tragedies of the era, portrayed by John Steinbeck in The Grapes of Wrath, *are locked in the nation's memory.*

What striking inconsistencies! How could they prevail?

During those dark years the strong feelings of elation and optimism that the Hillers recall were widespread among the large and growing numbers of citizens interested in the continent's wildlife populations, particularly game—the birds and mammals revered for sports hunting.

After World War I the number of hunters grew rapidly as new technologies and prosperous times brought automobiles and quality sporting arms within the reach of millions of Americans. In state after state the demand for game outdistanced the supply.

Beleaguered and bewildered, game administrators cut season lengths and bag limits, and with revenues from newly instituted license fees, boosted

budgets for law enforcement, predator control, and game farms.

As frustrations spread, a leading nationwide sportsmen's organization, the American Game Protective Association, formed a committee of fourteen—including scientists, educators, legislators, and able administrators—to review conditions and draft an American game policy to chart new directions. Its chairman, who also wrote the policy statement, was Aldo Leopold, a person uniquely qualified for the role. A well-educated professional forester with a distinguished career in the U.S. Forest Service, he had special interest and experience with wildlife resources, including leadership of New Mexico's sportsmen's association. Written in a clear and direct style that pulled no punches, the document proved an exceptionally useful set of guidelines. It was adopted at the Seventeenth American Game Conference in December 1930 and at once became the pattern for remarkable progress in the decade to follow. Something of the policy's dynamic and far-reaching qualities are revealed in this quotation from its pages:

NEED OF FACTS, SKILL, AND FUNDS
Cover, food, and protection (i.e., management) do not increase game unless they are of the right kind. Game management may be unduly expensive unless skillfully dovetailed with the management of the primary crop.

To select the right kind of management and to apply it skillfully requires biological facts and men who can advise the landowner how to apply them.

The facts must be discovered and the men trained. In short, game management must be recognized as a distinct profession and developed accordingly.

All these actions will require large additional funds, both public and private.

Two Hillers remember well some of the conditions in game administration in New York during the latter years of the 1920s. Money was becoming available, but informed direction from research and trained staff was still uncommon. First Art Hawkins comments on the effects of those conditions as he experienced them during the years he was growing up in Batavia and hunting the area's excellent farm country:

When I lived there, western New York was great pheasant country. I've counted well over a hundred in a single flock. Yet the hunting season lasted only four days—two successive Thursdays followed by two successive Saturdays. That was when game management was in its infancy, and the authorities had yet to learn that a four-day staggered season brings out far more hunters and kills far more birds than does a much longer but continuous hunting season. Such classics as Leopold's *Game Management* and Stoddard's *Bobwhite Quail* had not yet been published. Special game bird studies such as Ralph King's on ruffed grouse in Minnesota, Paul Errington's on quail in Wisconsin, and Howard Wight's on pheasants in Michigan were just getting started.

Also I grew up during a time when any sportsman worthy of the name shot "chicken hawks" and other "varmints" on sight. Once while I was hunting pheasants, a soaring red-tailed hawk flew too close, and I shot it, gloating that I had done my bit for conservation that day. Predator control and game farms were perceived as ways to achieve game abundance.

Ben Bradley provides an account of a game refuge development scheme that was being promoted as a panacea by some New York State game officials during those years: "The concept, which proved essentially false for New York, was quite simple: Buy cheap farmland (very abundant), post most or all of it against hunting, control predators (mostly by ground and pole traps), plant food patches, and voila! The game—native and stocked birds—would flourish and build up to benefit the surrounding lands for hunting." The scheme involved using hunting license proceeds to purchase and set up refuges in areas that had become marginal for farming. In fact, that was the origin of a thousand-acre refuge that existed on Connecticut Hill when the grouse survey began there in 1930.

Then, with the onset of the 1930s, game-conservation affairs began to change, with an astonishing rapidity. Still sensitive to that eruption of new ways, Art Hawkins uses this analogy: "During the early 1930s game management burst out all over the place like flowering crabs in spring, so the administrators who set the pheasant seasons of the late 1920s for my home territory shouldn't be judged too harshly."

Ben tells us how New York's refuge policy was challenged and changed by the knowledgeable and aggressive superintendent of the state's new Bureau of Game, Gardiner Bump:

Bump came along after the movement had started. He and others began to question its validity. But when Bump became superintendent of the Bureau of Game in the 1930s, he not only took game farms and game refuges under his wing, he seized on the opportunity offered by FDR's Resettlement Administration to get in on the ground floor and acquire more upland areas like Pharsalia and Connecticut Hill. He literally pounded and hammered to have his way in getting seventy thousand acres of the new game-management areas—coining such names for them as Hi-Tor, Rattlesnake Hill, Hanging Bog, and Happy Valley.

Bump was, shall we say, a driver. He pushed hard for the new profession of game management.

When Ben reminisces about Gardiner Bump's boundless energy, he mentions the time in 1933 when "as a junior in agricultural economics at Cornell I was privileged to go by auto with Bump, Edminster, and Darrow on a trip to several midwestern states for the purpose of contacting important contributors in the new field of game research and management. The highlight was a luncheon meeting with Aldo Leopold in Madison, Wisconsin—a high point in my life."

How formative and significant a year 1933 proved to be in the annals of wildlife conservation across all of North America! In March, Franklin D. Roosevelt was sworn in as president, foreshadowing many major advances in wildlife endeavors and all aspects of resource conservation.

The year also saw a giant step forward for formal wildlife education and professional development, in the publication of Aldo Leopold's text, Game Management. *The volume has proved a classic reference, not only on principles and practice, but also on the profession's philosophical foundation. Still in print and in use, it has served the discipline admirably for sixty years.*

Also noteworthy is that in 1933 Aldo Leopold was awarded a professorial chair in game management at the University of Wisconsin–Madison, the first such academic position anywhere.

Leopold's text and activities stimulated great interest across the continent. Where suitable teaching resources existed, the text soon became the basis for new courses, such as the one instituted in spring 1936 at Cornell by Arthur Allen and Frank Edminster. It was featured in the game-management part of a new five-part curriculum in wildlife conservation and management introduced by the College of Agriculture in fall 1935 (see facing page).

The opportunity to pursue graduate studies under Aldo Leopold's tutelage also became a widely sought goal. Two Cornellians soon were to become advanced-degree candidates in the program: Hiller Art Hawkins and Al Hochbaum.

Bill Severinghaus writes about one of the early students in Leopold's graduate program who came east for a "look-see" in the summer of 1936:

We had a visiting biologist during the summer. Doug Wade, a student of Leopold's from Madison, lived with us at the farmhouse and was on routine daily surveys for a couple of weeks. He was interested in all phases of the fieldwork and wanted to talk about our methods and observations. He talked with Frank Edminster, and because I had been on the survey for parts of two years, he was interested in my recollections. He also wanted to see the square slashings and the long, narrow ones that had been cut in the woods for habitat improvement. I was his guide; we walked and talked while visiting them. He was a friendly fellow, and we had a good time. We corresponded occasionally for a few years. I met him again at a Wildlife Society meeting.

In winter 1937 Ben joined a general conference for wildlife professionals held on the Cornell campus. It was a historic occasion. Turning to Ben's "trusty log" for that year, we have these two entries:

February 18—Ithaca. Room AZ and breakfast, 75¢; cigars, 10¢. To Fernow for game conference. First regional meeting of Society of Wildlife Specialists. Gave a ten-minute talk at conference. Lunch, 45¢. Afternoon game conference talks by Edminster, Gerstell, and others.

Banquet at Willard Straight, $1.25 (first banquet of a regional meeting of SWS).

February 19—Room AZ, 50¢; breakfast, 15¢. Game conference talks by Ernest Holt, Lithgow Osborne, Prof. Wright. Lunch, 35¢ (with G. Chase, W. Obenauf, R. Page). Then drove down to Cayuga Lake to see ducks—warm day, 50°, no snow. Afternoon lectures by A. A. Allen, Baker, Bell.

Ben's account of the first regional meeting of wildlife specialists in February 1937 at Cornell prompts some interesting observations about his list of attendees, brief though it is. As might be expected, there were students and faculty members present and state conservation agency workers in both technical and administrative capacities, including New York's commissioner, Lithgow Osborne. The diary entries also underscore the strength that northeastern leadership would contribute to the new professional organization—the Wildlife Society—that was to form later that same year. In fact, two men Ben names would be elected president of the society within the next four years: Arthur A. Allen became the organization's second president, and Richard Gerstell, game commission research biologist in Pennsylvania, its fifth.

Two historic days, and Ben still feels the excitement more than a half-century later: "Those days of 1937 were fresh, bright, and filled with much expectation!"

Preparation for Careers in Wildlife Conservation and Management

ORNITHOLOGY ◆ GAME-BIRD PROPAGATION ◆ GAME MANAGEMENT ◆ ECONOMIC ZOOLOGY AND ANIMAL ECOLOGY ◆ FISHERIES

Formal notice of the new program in wildlife conservation and management appeared in July 1935, in a twenty-page bulletin. It was a development of enduring significance. The program was described as follows:

The rapid extinction of many species of animals over large parts of their former ranges, noticeable especially during the past twenty-five years, shows the need of constructive measures of conservation.... The biological problems involved are altogether too complex to be solved without detailed scientific investigations.... This scientific basis for conservation has been growing, methods of artificial propagation formerly thought impossible have been perfected, and intricate problems of adjustment between species and their habitats have been elucidated until what is almost a new science has developed.

In organizing curricula for prospective workers in wild-life conservation and management, the attempt has been made to give

> CORNELL UNIVERSITY
> OFFICIAL PUBLICATION
> Volume XXVII   Number 2
>
> New York State
> College of Agriculture
>
> Announcement of Courses in
> Wild-Life Conservation
> and Management
> for 1935-36
>
> Ithaca, New York
> Published by the University
> July 15, 1935

◆ *The title page of the July 1935 announcement of the new program.*

the student not only a knowledge of present-day procedures but also a good background of training in the various sciences in which the basic facts and principles have been developed. Workers in conservation must cross the boundary lines of the conventionally organized biological sciences, and progress will be made by those who are themselves broadly trained and who can cooperate with specialists in the contributing fields. It is for this reason also that some of the instruction is given cooperatively by members of the staff of the University.

While not heretofore definitely organized as a curriculum in conservation, most of courses have long been available at Cornell University, and much of the pioneer research has been done at this institution. The out-of-doors, field phases, of biological work, always strongly emphasized at Cornell, are especially needed in the training of those interested in the conservation and management of wild life. The location of the University is favorable to this type of work.

This description of the course Professor Allen and Frank Edminster developed appeared in the announcement. The four New York State Conservation Department staff members named served as participating lecturers. In all, there were eleven members of that staff listed among the fifty instructors in the program in wildlife conservation and management.

Game Management. Second term. Credit three hours. Prerequisite, Botany 13 and Ornithology 126 or 131. Lecture, Th 10. McGraw 5. Laboratory and field work, S 8–1, and at least four all-day Saturday trips. McGraw, South Museum. Professor Allen and Messrs. Bump, Edminster, Skiff, and Darrow.

The principles and practices of game management as applied to field, woodland, forest, and aquatic game. Consideration of the properties and measurement of game populations, of the factors controlling abundance, of management technic, and of developmental plans for individual species. Laboratory studies of game species, predators, cover maps, management plans, feeding devices, and so on. Field work includes demonstrations and practice in game surveys, research methods, and other game-management practices. Laboratory fee, $3.

In recognition of Dick Reynolds's thirty-seven years of exemplary service as foreman, the Ithaca Game Farm was renamed in his honor in 1974. Dick (right) shared his day with his wife, Lois, Commissioner James L. Biggane, and family, colleagues, and friends.

CHAPTER ELEVEN

After the Hill

LEAVING CORNELL AND MOVING ON

AFTER GRADUATION the men who had participated in the grouse study took various paths. Some found jobs, even during America's Great Depression. Some went on to graduate school. And the conflagration of World War II drew many into military service. Their experiences on Connecticut Hill had imbued their abilities afield with resourcefulness, powers of observation, and good humor.

Ben Bradley's connection as a Hiller led to a career in public service in New York State. He entered that service on the ground floor:

Upon graduation in June 1934 I immediately left for Letchworth State Park in the Genesee River Valley to make a game cover map, a two-week assignment. I reported to Gardiner Bump in Albany. Bump kept me busy, knowing that federal funds might be available for federal land through Guy Rexford Tugwell's Resettlement Administration. I spent the rest of 1934 and most of 1935 scurrying around checking out possible purchases and cover-mapping. Greenleaf T. Chase came over from Massachusetts looking for work. Bump hired him, and Greenie helped me with mapmaking in the Albany office of the Conservation Department.

My appointment book says: "Ben O. Bradley, Spencer, NY; Game Specialist, Resettlement Administration, Division of Land Development, LD-NY-5; appointment received Nov. 18, 1935 @ $2,300 per year." Quite a raise from my $125 a month under Bump—with the title of game farm helper. Bump had sort of an understanding with the Resettlement people that I was "on loan," and I reported often to Bump, even though I worked out of the Binghamton RA office at 64 Henry Street (L. L. Huddleston was project manager). Our collective job was to get people to work on the various new sites being acquired; 2,400 men was the goal.

Bump insisted that each site have a trained biologist or forester who would see to it that as much of the work as possible would benefit wildlife. He often quarreled with state foresters over policy and practices. One of my jobs was to OK the hiring of "game technicians." Hirings included Bob Perry on site 5, Dansville; Glenn Morton on site 6, Naples; W. Obenauf on site 7, Pulaski; Greenie Chase on site 11, Shinhopple and Downsville.

After my ten-week stint—January 18 to April 5, 1935—conducting the Moose River Deer Investigation, Bump assigned me to help with locating and cover-mapping sites he expected would become LD-NY-5 project areas. He had the influence to see that I got the appointment in charge of the game-management work on all sites, using development plans he initiated, and employing 2,400 men, with all sites operating in 1936.

I spent some time on site 7, Happy Valley, Pulaski. I was the acting site superintendent for more than 250 men. In June 1938 my job was terminated, and foresters handled all activities. So from June until Pittman-Robertson funds were approved, I did miscellaneous work. One of those jobs was as a soil tester with the Farm Bureau in Steuben County. Bump called me to Albany in December 1938. I was assigned a Pittman-Robertson pheasant research project. (Dirck Benson came on as researcher on waterfowl.) I did not stay with the research project much more than a year. Bump "dreamed up" the

district game manager concept and succeeded in getting three men established for the whole state, and later four: Asa Smith, northern and northeastern New York; Bob Perry, western New York, headquarters in Rochester; Al Bromley in eastern New York and the Hudson Valley, headquarters in Poughkeepsie; and I, central New York, headquarters in Syracuse.

The landowner-sportsman public-hunting program (leased land for public hunting) was a major new program then. I had three of those areas to supervise. In 1940 one of the ardent Hillers, Earl Westervelt, helped me run the check station on the Cayuga County landowner-sportsman area. It was a worthwhile program, but it was dropped after the war. The costs were too great to justify it.

Royce Brower graduated from Cornell in 1933 but later came back for an additional year. After the 1936–37 school year he began the job of running the grouse survey in the Adirondack study area near Elizabethtown:

I boarded with Bob Darrow. While there, I took a federal civil service exam for junior biologist and did reasonably well. But come fall, back to whatever I could find—threshing crews, silo filling, and so on.

In February 1938 Brookfield, New York, needed a vo-ag teacher. I got there first. I stayed until 1939, when I was suddenly notified that I could be a junior biologist at a CCC camp in New Jersey, working with a new soil conservation district. That's how the Soil Conservation Service became my career, although for only two years as a biologist. They thought I should be a soil conservationist. And so I was, in Maryland, until Uncle Sam thought I should be in uniform.

Greenleaf Chase's work on Connecticut Hill was actually one of his early jobs, and what he learned from Ben Bradley led to another job:

Ben Bradley's instructions and teachings of cover-type mapping paid off, for I got a summer job the next year—1936—with the Resettlement Administration. It eventually paid an enormous salary of $5 per day. Mapping was done on unwieldy property maps supplied through Gardiner Bump's office. I didn't know I was working for the RA until I got bitten by a dog that also bit the postman. It tried to bite a state trooper also but got shot, so I knew it would be safe to finish my mapping on that property as soon as I could walk again. Anyway, an RA supervisor caught up with me, and I signed some payrolls and was instructed to report to the old Ithaca courthouse.

I had a wonderful field summer, staying at farmhouses for a dollar a day with breakfast and supper, meeting interesting people, and briefly joining their lives. I would select a farmhouse by cruising until I saw one with an excellent vegetable garden and strawberry patch. Boy, there's nothing like homemade ice cream with fresh crushed strawberries.

The grouse survey figured prominently in Walt Crissey's life and career. He began working on the survey as a Boy Scout while still in high school. His responsibilities increased, he became one of the authors of the published work, and his interesting and distinguished career began to take shape:

I graduated in June 1937 and was placed in charge of the summer survey on Connecticut Hill at the usual salary of $100 a month. As I recall, Eddie Edminster left the New York State Conservation Department to take a position with the U.S. Soil Conservation Service on July 1, and I was both surprised and gratified when I was appointed to fill his position. The salary was $2,600 a year, which doesn't sound like much now but was well above average for a new graduate in 1937.

The primary duties were to continue the Connecticut Hill survey and to initiate the overall summary and analysis of the voluminous field data that had accumulated. In 1940, when it became apparent that the United States might be drawn into the war, Bump decided that some of us should "have our brains picked." Whatever knowledge we had should be reduced to words and figures before we either enlisted or were drafted.

Bump was a hard taskmaster. He expected a lot, but jobs were hard to come by, and besides,

◆ *As Adirondack deer investigations got under way in the early 1930s, Vernon Bailey, chief field naturalist with the U.S. Biological Survey and an eminent mammalogist, was asked to make an inspection trip and offer suggestions. Bob Darrow took him to various field sites. Bailey took this photograph of Bob and a local woodsman, Tommy Simonds, on April 19, 1932, near Eagle Bay.*

the work was interesting. For about two years I reported to the Albany office at 8:30 Monday morning, left at 4:30 Friday afternoon, and was responsible for the Connecticut Hill survey on weekends. I was assigned to write several sections of the book and analyze much of the data pertaining to the rest of the book. It was a grind, and I must confess, there were some weekends when I drove the crew to the Hill in the morning, returned to Ithaca, and picked them up in the afternoon. Although the grouse book was not published until after the war, most of the work was done before I enlisted in October 1942 as a navy pilot.

Ransom Page was in a good position to get a job after graduation:

I learned the Resettlement Administration had given New York several game-management sites scattered across the state. Owing to my experience on the Hill, I was right in line to work on those areas, such as Happy Valley, Hi-Tor, Rattlesnake Hill, and Hanging Bog. So I mapped several of them myself and served as temporary superintendent in a couple of instances.

Gene Gerberg, a 1939 graduate who had majored in entomology, remained at Cornell to pursue a Master of Science degree in that field. By the time his advanced degree was conferred, he had landed a position with the Conservation Department to perform essential laboratory work related to the grouse investigation. For Gene the early 1940s were action-packed years:

I believe it was in the spring of 1940, after I finished work on my M.S., that John C. Jones interviewed me at Cornell, and I became the entomologist for the research lab located at the state game farm at Delmar. I guess I was *the* entomologist for the Conservation Department, as I don't think there was any other. My job was to receive the grouse stomachs that guys like Mac Blue collected, separate out the insects and seeds, and identify the insect fragments. Johnny handled the seeds.

Joe Dell worked for E. L. Cheatum and Cleon Goble in the parasitology lab. We both lived in the old CCC barracks on the game farm. Our salary was $100 a month. Sometime in the fall of 1940 Johnny Jones, Joe, and I moved into an apartment in Delmar. As one of the junior members of the group, I was assigned to drive the bus into Albany

◆ *Time out to bury Joe Dell in the snow during winter 1940–41, when Gene Gerberg (left), Joe, and Johnny Jones shared an apartment while doing research for the Conservation Department in Delmar.*

to pick up the workers for the game farm. As I had never driven a car until that summer, you can imagine how scared I was to drive a bus in snow and ice. I managed to survive, and eventually someone else took over the route.

Johnny Jones got married, and when he moved out, I think John Whalen moved in. In June 1941 I married Jo Betty Vick, a Cornell '41 entomologist. Jo Betty and I found a large apartment in Delmar, and John Whalen moved in with us. Sometime in early fall, we moved out to the foot of the Helderbergs (I believe it was in Unionville). We rented an apartment for $10 a month and sublet one room to Chuck Mason. Of course there was no running water, and we used an outhouse.

We had some good times at the game farm!

In October 1941 I received a telegram from the U.S. Public Health Service offering me a job, which I accepted. Six entomologists were recruited, and after Pearl Harbor we made up the Malaria

Control in War Areas program. The program later became the famous CDC (Centers for Disease Control) in Atlanta.

Joe Dell and I used to get a kick out of the fact that he and I were eventually commissioned, while our bosses in the Conservation Department ended up as enlisted personnel.

Like Gene, Mason Lawrence played a significant support role in the preparation of the grouse report after earning an advanced degree:

I was asked by the chairman of my Ph.D. committee, Professor Mottley, to accept a position as a biometrician with the Bureau of Game to assist with the report of the grouse survey. Accordingly, from 1941 to 1943 I worked in that capacity in Albany, joining three of the authors of the tome—Gardiner Bump, Bob Darrow, and Walt Crissey—in work on the analysis and presentation of data gathered in the course of the entire investigation. After that work was completed, I served in the U.S. Navy for three years. Then, in 1946, I returned to the Conservation Department and began a series of positions ranging from regional fisheries biologist to deputy commissioner, my post at retirement in 1974. It was a rewarding career and one I thoroughly enjoyed.

The Civilian Conservation Corps provided thousands of young men with shelter, three square meals a day, and a variety of work experiences. Don Schierbaum served as a camp foreman in the CCC after he completed his two semesters of postgraduate study at Cornell in 1938–39, and he eventually found himself back on the Hill again:

In June 1939 Gardiner Bump offered me a job in a CCC camp in the Capital District Refuge for $2,000 a year. I accepted the position, for that was a good wage (schoolteachers started at $600 to $800). In the CCC camp room rent was $5 a month, and board was $15 a month. There was no income tax or social security taken out of the check. We were paid $146 on the last day of the month.

I was expected to select and train a crew to do grouse surveys on the refuge. The CCC boys were paid $1 a day, or $30 a month. Of that amount, $5 went to the enrollees, and $25 went to their families. A common saying was: "Another day, another dollar. A million days, a million dollars."

My first crew was from New York City. Needless to say, they were useless in the woods. Most of my time was spent locating lost crew members. We also had a few men from rural Virginia. After convincing the supervisor that those men were essential to a successful survey, I picked six of them. I drove the crew to work in a pickup truck, and that made us independent of the other crews. After completing the summer survey, we were transferred to stream improvement under Dave Cook. He marked the location where we were to build straight-log dams and bank cribbings to hold the Kinderhook Creek in its banks. We built the various structures out of hemlock and stone. They are still present and working today.

The camp was transferred to Cornell's Arnot Forest in October 1939. From that base, we worked on the grouse survey in five of the Connecticut Hill sections: 15, 16, 17, 20N, and 20S. We worked Monday through Friday. The college crews worked the same sections on weekends.

The CCC crew did not enjoy cold weather or snowshoes. The army issued oversize shoes and five-buckle overshoes. They were cumbersome and made walking on snowshoes difficult. The hardest time was late February and March. The snow would melt during the day and freeze at night. That put a glaze on top that would support a man's weight but made travel on the slopes treacherous. In some cases we played Tarzan and swung from one tree to the next to maintain our footing. As the day warmed up, the snow would melt, and the rawhide webbing on the snow shoes would sag and pick up four or five inches of snow at every step. It was tough going, but the CCC crew members gave a good account of themselves!

During the winter and spring survey the CCC crew picked up six dead grouse with no apparent injuries. Autopsies found that they had all died of broken necks. During the spring survey one of the

CCC crew members came out of the woods with a male grouse sitting on his finger. The bird had been sitting on a drumming log and hadn't flushed. It made no effort to escape and appeared normal. The bird was sent to Delmar for examination. It had a bruise on its back and one lung was completely filled with blood.

After graduation Art Hawkins went on to graduate school. His description of that period of his life includes a who's who of American conservation:

The Hill experience paid off handsomely. It helped me become Prof. Aldo Leopold's third graduate student at the University of Wisconsin.

The summer after I graduated from Cornell, in 1934, I worked for the state on Dr. Emmeline Moore's stream survey of the Hudson-Mohawk watershed. Partly as a result of that happy experience and rejuvenated finances, I returned to Cornell as an M.S. candidate in fisheries under Dr. George Embody. But it soon became apparent that the path I was taking would lead to a career in a fish hatchery. That wasn't what I wanted, so I got back in touch with Bill Hamilton and Dr. Allen.

Late in 1934 Aldo Leopold contacted Dr. Allen about an opening for a research assistant that he wanted to fill as soon as possible. About the same time a job offer came from the Audubon society to study the ivory-billed woodpecker. Jim Tanner, a Ph.D. candidate, and I were both available. Jim had

◆ *The date: June 23, 1955. The place: A meadow on Connecticut Hill that was once part of the Boylan farm. The remains of the barn, across the road from the house, can be seen in the background. The occasion: The fifth annual meeting of Cornell's Sportsmen's Conservation Workshop, a statewide educational event for sportsman-conservationist leaders founded in 1951 by Prof. Gustav Swanson (at right with a Scandinavian bull-moose-calling horn, which he is using to assemble participants). Paul Kelsey (standing tall in khakis), then local district game manager and responsible for the Connecticut Hill Game Management Area, is discussing the effects of forest regrowth on wildlife and his agency's efforts to maintain habitat diversity.*

first pick and chose the Audubon job. I packed my things, and on January 2, 1935, at 8:30 a.m., I walked into the office of the "father of game management," Aldo Leopold, to begin the greatest experience that a wildlife student could possibly have. That he had selected me seemed almost too good to be true. I suspect that the entry on my

résumé indicating that I had worked on the grouse survey had a lot to do with it, along with the recommendations from Dr. Allen and Dr. Hamilton. Later I learned that both of them were highly regarded by Professor Leopold.

My first assignment in Wisconsin was to study the quail irruption. Quail, evidently responding to a series of mild winters, had spread throughout the southern half of Wisconsin in great numbers. I was supposed to document the spread and identify the reasons. One problem: the quail was a new bird to me. But the Hiller experience paid off. Whether grouse, pheasants, or quail, the same basic study techniques apply. Later I was to add Hungarian partridges and prairie chickens to the list of upland game birds I studied, using the same general approaches.

Some months into my work in Wisconsin, Dr. Arthur Allen came to Madison on a lecture tour. Early the next morning I took him to the Faville Grove Wildlife Experimental Area, which I managed and where a remnant flock of prairie chickens still conducted their courtship ritual. While walking across the prairie near the booming ground, we flushed a chicken from her nest, while a delighted Dr. Allen filmed. That was probably the last nest on that prairie. Shortly thereafter the prairie became a cornfield, and the chickens were gone forever.

After obtaining my M.S. degree from the University of Wisconsin, in 1938, I joined the Illinois National History Survey until World War II interrupted. My work in Illinois mostly involved waterfowl and wetland habitat.

Neal Kuhn left Cornell before he graduated:

I was stupid for not pushing for a third year at Cornell. Knowing what I know now, I would have

done that. But I went on with my schooling in wildlife at North Carolina State at Raleigh with Dr. Ross Stevens. I soon ran out of funds because of the extra tuition charged to nonresidents.

I spent the winter in Florida and practically lived in the Everglades (which, by the way, are very different now) with a friend I developed at the University of Miami. I enjoyed the screaming of the limpkins, among many other things.

Spring of 1940 found me working at the tree and shrub nursery at Painted Post and Big Flats, New York. I stayed with that until fall, when I entered Syracuse in forestry and wildlife. There I worked toward a B.S. degree under more good profs.

Spring of 1942, still on the way to a degree, I worked part-time with the Tennessee Valley Authority mapping with aerial photos and making new U.S. Geological Survey sheets.

Those drawn into military service were schooled there in the unique lessons of the pursuits of war. Many undertook positions of leadership. The "tuition" was high. At least one lost his life, one became a prisoner of war, and several were wounded.

John Whalen became an army major in the South Pacific and, despite shrapnel wounds, served subsequently as a New York State Conservation Department manager.

Ben Bradley enlisted in the U.S. Navy and began service at the Sampson Base. His history as a Cornell athlete may have resulted in his assignment as a physical-training instructor. One of his fellow

physical-training instructors was an aspiring young actor, Henry Fonda. Ben's naval days were terminated before the end of hostilities, when navy doctors found he had lingering effects from a childhood bout with rheumatic fever. He then returned to the Conservation Department.

Royce Brower also had a military job for which he was well qualified:

Thanks to my work in soil conservation, I got a break in World War II. The army air force decided they wanted men with experience in work with aerial photos, and I qualified to go in as a second lieutenant. I was a photo interpreter with a B-25 bomb group in the Pacific and eventually with the Joint Intelligence Center at Pearl Harbor. With the bomb group I was at Tarawa and Makin islands. Afterwards we went back to Hawaii to prepare for Okinawa and what might follow. I spent two months in a hospital with arthritis, which led to my transfer to the Intelligence Center. At separation time I signed up for the reserves, and I stayed in until retirement, at age sixty.

For Neal Kuhn as well, experience with aerial photography led to intelligence work:

In summer 1942 I got a commission in the navy as an ensign assigned to photographic intelligence. I went on active duty that fall. I was in the service until 1946. I was sent to China through India and over the "hump" in the Himalayas. We were the "rice paddy navy," procuring information from Gen. Claire Chennault of the Fourteenth U.S. Air Force. It was quite an experience.

Art Hawkins spent the war years in the veterinary service:

Military duty spanned four and a half years as a member of the veterinary service. While stationed in Texas, helping develop a milk shed for several army posts, I had ample opportunity to get well acquainted with the high-plains country and the high productivity of its playa lakes during wet years. One time Bill Hamilton came to Amarillo on an inspection trip for the air corps. I took him on a field trip to a playa lake well populated with shorebirds. We found the nest of an avocet, and he remarked, "Now I can die happy."

Chuck Mason became a "guest" of the German government:

After graduation, in 1941, I was employed by the NYS Conservation Department. There I worked on the statewide waterfowl program until called to active duty by the army air corps. After training as a navigator, I was commissioned second lieutenant and assigned to the Eighth Air Force, flying heavy bombers out of England. I was shot down

◆ *An introspective Sergeant Spittler writing a letter home in April 1941, back at the Fort McClellan barracks after maneuvers in Tennessee. "There's no question about it now," he admitted. "I should have taken Advanced Drill."*

near Berlin on my ninth mission and served nine months as a POW until our camp was liberated by Russian troops.

Even in the army, Jim Otis had reunions with Hillers and Cornellians:

While stationed at cold, wet Jefferson Barracks, on the Mississippi River near St. Louis, I decided to get out of the mud of our tent area. I wandered over to

the permanent party area of nice, comfortable-looking brick barracks. Lo and behold, I ran into Al Jerome, a bona fide Hiller. As you can imagine, we had quite a get-together.

The summer of 1942 I was stationed at Chanute Field, near Champaign-Urbana. It was quite a treat for the GIs to attend the dances at the University of Illinois. I happened to get in on a real fancy one—with a receiving line yet. Who should be handing out punch and cookies but Prof. J. Nelson Spaeth, formerly in Cornell's Department of Forestry. I had worked for him my freshman year, when I was still thinking about forestry as a career. He was teaching and had the title of state forester.

Don Spittler became a colonel in the U.S. Army Reserve. But he recalls an earlier day as a foot soldier, when a Connecticut Hill buddy got the last laugh:

My most cherished memories include events and experiences associated with Cornell. Most of them were pleasant and exhilarating, but not my bout with ROTC. Since I was allergic to wool, the uniform caused me great discomfort, especially around the neck and in the breeches, which were laced inside knee-high leather boots. The irksome task of donning the uniform and sweating out the drill period made me a dissenter, and my attitude resulted in having to repeat Basic at the end of my sophomore year—a bitter pill to swallow. John Whalen, my section leader on the Hill, went on to take Advanced Drill. We had numerous debates about the merits of ROTC, and every time I met him on campus, wearing his cadet uniform, I would offer a taunting remark and laugh.

Soon after graduation the war clouds drifting over Europe prompted the activation of the national guard. I promptly enlisted in the Twenty-seventh Division in October 1940, under the agreement that I would be released at the end of one year with immunity from the forthcoming draft. Never trust the government. The following summer, when our unit was in Tennessee on maneuvers, it was announced that all of us were in for the duration of the emergency plus six months. Naturally we felt betrayed, and esprit de corps was shattered.

Then came John's day for retaliation. On a sweltering afternoon, with full pack and a Springfield rifle slung over my shoulder, I was in a long line of troops marching down a dusty road. An oncoming weapons carrier appeared, and we were ordered to deploy to the side of the road. As it approached me, I noticed the gold bars of a second lieutenant, who was standing above the windshield. And then I recognized the shavetail; it was John Whalen. I shouted, "Hey, John!" and when he spotted me, he roared with laughter and yelled, "Don't you wish you had taken Advanced Drill?"

Don Foley describes his unexpected post-graduate career:

I'd been out of Cornell for only a year, working with Dirck Benson in Delmar on the waterfowl project, when the draft called, and I had to go. I wasn't mustered out until September 1945, after the Japanese surrendered.

First it was boot camp at Camp Lee, Virginia, where I ran into Joe Dell. Actually, it was in Richmond that Joe almost ran over me. And I almost got to see him later in North Africa, Sicily, and Italy. We each knew the other guy's outfit was nearby but made no contact. In conditions like that it was no wonder.

After Camp Lee it was maneuvers in North Carolina, where I joined my "real" outfit, a part of the First Amphibious Engineer Brigade, stationed in Camp Edwards, Massachusetts.

Then in spring of 1942 it was over to the British Isles, where we joined a naval base in Scotland and later motored down to the south of England, where we maneuvered on the English Channel.

That fall we took off for the invasion of North Africa, coming ashore at Oran. Rommel gave the Allies fits there for some time, and it wasn't until the summer of 1943 that we were able to move east to Tunisia and then invade Sicily. In late summer we took off from the north shore of Sicily and invaded Italy at Salerno. (We were getting pretty good by then.) North of Naples things bogged down in the fall, then winter mud set in, stiffening German resistance. Rather than use us in crossing the Volturno, the command called for us to back off, get on the "banana boat," and go back to Great Britain. That was a nice change after all the sand, palm trees, and languages we couldn't speak. I even found time and a way to attend Oxford for a week.

But bad things awaited us, and D day in June found us fighting our way into Normandy. Slowly we leapfrogged east, but as winter settled in again, we hadn't yet gotten past Luxembourg or over the Rhine. (That's what they were gonna use us for!) The Germans had changed their counterattack plans greatly, and back to the coast we went and to Great Britain once more. Soon we were headed back to the States, and if the point system hadn't come out then, they'd have used us in invading Japan.

As it was, we stayed on the West Coast (Fort Lewis) until we were sent back to Fort Dix, New Jersey, and mustered out in September 1945.

Longest damn picnic I was ever on!

Whether or not they participated in the war, Hillers survived difficult times and moved on to leave prints of leadership in their professions. Those who survived the war did so without losing the positive outlook that had been evident in their days with the grouse study.

A HILLER LOOKS BACK

NICK DRAHOS

FOR CONSERVATION educator-writer Nick Drahos, looking back is second nature—a trait of character—all part of his lifelong searching. In his look back he shares a panorama of his life as a Hiller.

I came to Cornell in a roundabout way and became a wildlife biologist and a conservation educator in an even more roundabout way. Being a high school football and basketball all-star, I was wooed mightily by seventeen colleges and universities, including Columbia, Fordham, Villanova, West Point, Annapolis, Bucknell, Cornell, and a host of lesser but nice colleges. They all offered scholarships, but there was a catch. They wanted to examine the goods. That meant I had to travel to their campuses to butt heads with their football teams. I had to scrimmage against the best they could throw at me, but I managed to hold my own. The best part was that after I was done, they still offered me scholarships.

However, the choice of a college was not easy, for I did not have a career in mind. I didn't want a city college, so that eliminated Columbia and Fordham.

I detested the regimentation of the army and the navy, and I did not want to take business administration or theology. I wanted to be a scientist of sorts, if I could, and have variety in course work and country scenery.

I was born on a farm, raised in a rural sort of a city in Pennsylvania (Ford City), where I ran barefooted for nine years of my life before they caught me and fitted me with shoes, and came from a hunting family. I liked Cornell, even though the Columbia University School of Journalism appealed to me, as I liked writing. I dreamed of being a famous world-trotting journalist, a forester, a chemist, and a bunch of other things, and I always envied kids that actually wanted to be lawyers or doctors or something specific. Curiosity was my forte, and it was also my undoing. I liked to do everything, and I was good at most, but I never fell in love with a career. The grass was greener elsewhere—always.

I picked Cornell, not because of its football team but because it looked like a university should look, and the surroundings reminded me of my hometown. It was out in the country, the campuses were gracious (much prettier than today), and it had several colleges within its system, so if I didn't like one career, I could switch to another college without completely switching the scenery. What to study was the problem. To be a farmer, I needed a farm, and I did not have one. In desperation I signed up for dairy industry, thinking I could become a bacteriologist or something. The main thing was to go to college, anyhow. I could figure out a career later.

So I registered, got my courses lined up, and returned to my $3-a-week room on Summit Place in Collegetown. Everything was in turmoil. Stork Sanford wanted me to go out for crew. Bo Rowland wanted me for basketball. And then there was baseball. "Nope," I said, "football's enough. I came here to study and not to play around." I almost went out for the fencing team though. I had read *The Three Musketeers* when I was a kid.

So how did I get into the field of wildlife and fisheries management?

On the third floor of my rooming house I met a junior named Gordon "Pappy" Leversee. I asked him what he was majoring in. He said, "Wildlife management." I nearly flipped. I didn't know that Cornell offered a program in wildlife management, let alone fisheries management. Right then I changed horses, and I never got off.

Aldo Leopold had nothing to do with my taking up conservation work. I had never heard of the guy, although his book gave Cornell an excuse to set up a conservation curriculum. I would have taken it even if Max Podunk espoused it, for I had become imbued with the love of nature and the animals therein when I was a mere five-year-old running barefooted in the hills of Pennsylvania, searching for crayfish in damp spots.

The next morning I went to Barton Hall, a combination indoor sports and ROTC arena, to find Dr. A. A. Allen sitting at a desk. I handed him my first-term schedule and asked if he would be my advisor. He looked at me owlishly through his glasses and then down at my course list, signed his initials, and said yes. That's how I became what I became—whatever I became. I still don't know what. Would you believe it? I'm still searching for a career.

Leversee told me about the Connecticut Hill grouse survey and said they'd be hiring students in the spring for about fifty cents an hour. I could work weekends and could make four bucks a day, and football would not interfere. I needed the money. I was probably one of the poorest students that Cornell had ever had. I arrived with twenty-five bucks—my football scholarship paid the tuition, and my room, books, and fees (about 170 bucks) were paid by an alumnus (bless his heart!). All I had to do was work for my meals, study, and play football well enough to stay in school. Still not knowing if I wanted to be a wildlife biologist or a fisheries manager, I took all the courses in both

A Brilliant Football Player

Allison Danzig, the New York Times's *veteran sportswriter, wrote about Nick's football career:*

Drahos' stature as a linesman has hardly been surpassed by any other Cornellian, though at 6 feet 3 and 212 pounds he was not as big as some of the others. For three years he was a standout at tackle, unusually fast, quick and agile for his size. Drahos excelled as a placekicker, and he was a stabilizing force and diagnostician on the field.

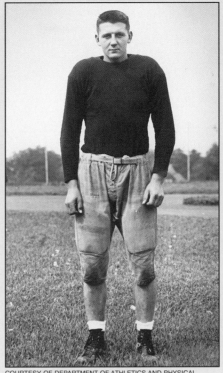

COURTESY OF DEPARTMENT OF ATHLETICS AND PHYSICAL EDUCATION, CORNELL UNIVERSITY

Nick's efforts from 1938 to 1940 helped his team to a 19–3–1 record overall. In 1939 Cornell was 8–0, winning over Penn State and Ohio State. He is a member of the National College Football Hall of Fame and the Cornell Athletic Hall of Fame. Nick was one of our best two-way linemen of all time—an extraordinary athlete.

◆ *An offensive and defensive tackle and a placekicker, Nick was named a first-team all-American in 1939 and 1940.*

fields, hedging my bets so I could get a job in either field when I graduated. Wildlife biology won out because of a job offer.

What do I remember of Connecticut Hill? Steep hills, the tail ends of flying grouse, trying to keep straight survey lines by guiding on the man on your right and yelling "Grouse! Male!," and a bunch of nice, wacky guys (later I found them to be dedicated and talented). I remember trying to sleep in the cabin built by Works Progress Administration men. They did a nice job, but it had a huge fireplace

that didn't throw heat more than six inches into the freezing room.

It is rumored that I asked Gardiner Bump, Walt Crissey, and Bob Darrow (our leaders): "Suppose you can't see the tail of the grouse as it flies to determine whether it's a male or a female? What do you do?" "Well, Nick," Gardiner is supposed to have said after consulting with the other two, "in that case, you spit in your left palm and strike the spit with your right index finger. If the spittle flies to the left,

◆ *In real wilderness style, with pot dangling from his pack, Nick pauses along the trail to a brook trout pond in the Adirondack backcountry. Fishing for trout and bow hunting for whitetails are among Nick's favorite pastimes.*

it's a male. If it goes to the right, it's a female!" Is that how and why the book *The Ruffed Grouse* is so accurate in its identification? Did everybody practice the spittle technique and come up with the same accurate identifications?

I graduated in June 1941 with honors in grouse identification. As I recall, I knew 99 percent of the Hillers. Many of them I went to class with, and those who had "groused" before me I worked with after I got out of college.

Course work at Cornell was under world-class teachers, although we did not know it at the time: zoologists A. H. Wright, W. J. Hamilton, Jr., William B. Senning, A. A. Allen, Peter Paul Kellogg (sound and photography), Ed Raney, Perry Gilbert, and Bob Eadie; rural educators E. Laurence Palmer and Eva Gordon; foresters A. B. Recknagel and Cedric Guise; and botanists W. C. Muenscher and Karl Wiegand. In fisheries there was Archie Hess, C. W. Mottley, and the granddaddy of fisheries management, George C. Embody. And of course there was the dry humor of Bristow Adams.

I think I managed to take every one of their courses, a total of about 132 hours, except Mottley's statistics classes. They did not agree with me.

I stopped to see Doc Wright and his wife, Anna, whenever I could. They always seemed to be revising or publishing an opus on frogs or a book on the Okefenokee Swamp. He even conned me into buying one. I can still see his twinkling blue eyes. He was truly a scientist and a teacher of the old school.

I also stopped in to see Doc Hamilton at least once a year until his death. We used to ice-fish together on Oneida Lake, and I even got into one or two poker games with him in NYS's Constantia boathouse.

Another professor that I saw much of was E. Laurence Palmer. We had a nice friendship, and I had fun with his family after field trips and on visits to the house.

I got to know Doc Allen quite well after college days. Many didn't know that Doc was an avid duck hunter. I stayed at his house two weeks of every year during the late-winter duck seasons in the 1950s and 1960s, hunting with him, his son David, and John Carver (who married Doc's daughter Connie) almost up to the time of his death. I remember lying in the snow in cornfields waiting for the geese and ducks to come into our decoy spread. Ofttimes we'd lie there counting the lone migrating loons flying overhead while Doc sang, "Massa's in the cold, cold ground." His death was quite a jolt to me, as was the death of his wife, Elsa, which followed shortly. I had privileged moments with some of my favorite professors.

Of course World War II intervened. It took four years out of my life and everybody else's. I got out of the army on 31 December 1945 and returned to New York in spring 1946, looking for a job. I found none, so I called Dr. E. L. Palmer at Cornell and asked if he had room for an M.S. candidate in conservation education. He said, "Yes, come on up." Somewhere along the line I had taken a civil service exam for assistant game research investigator at the NYS Delmar Research Center to work with Bill Severinghaus on the white-tailed deer. I had forgotten about it, but in June 1946 I got a telegram asking if I wanted the deer-research job for the magnificent sum of $2,715 a year. Did God make little green apples? The master's could wait. I could go back later to do it (and I did, in 1956).

I worked with Bill for three months and enjoyed the camaraderie of E. L. Cheatum, Asa Smith, Don Foley, Chuck Mason, Dirck Benson, Jack Tanck, Mason Lawrence, Ralph Smith, Joe Dell, and Art Cook at the lab; and Vic Skiff, Dr. William B. Senning (formerly an anatomy professor from Cornell), Clayt Seagears, Gardiner Bump, Bob Darrow, Cecil Heacox, P. W. Fosburg, Fred Everett (an artist), Al Hall, Earl Westervelt, and Al Bromley and many foresters, park people, engineers, and fisheries people at the Albany office. Many of those people were former Hillers.

A catastrophe occurred in my wife's family (I had married the farmer's daughter years before), and I quit to run her family's seven-hundred-acre crop-dairy farm in Aurora, New York, in December 1946. The lab boys all cried when I left, they were so happy.

I ran the farm through September 1947 and then decided I wanted to be a veterinarian specializing in wildlife diseases. I came to the Cornell vet school in the fall of 1947 and stayed one year, until I got another telegram, this time from the new NYS Division of Conservation Education, asking if I wanted

to be a pioneer conservation-education assistant at $3,765 a year. I did, and I gave up my veterinary career and never looked back.

At the division I wrote for the *New York State Conservationist* magazine, illustrating it with my art and photos; traveled the state and worked with schools, trying to get conservation-education concepts integrated into their curricula; made a dozen feature movies on wildlife and education; and helped organize and run the Boys Conservation Camps. I told everyone that I hunted and fished for a living and got paid for it. What more could a fellow ask?

Well, to make a long story short, I ended up spending twenty-two years in the division. I became nationally noted for my writings and motion pictures, but fame is ephemeral. Now no one knows me for the work I did. They only know of my football fame, which includes being inducted into the National College Football Hall of Fame. Come to think of it, not many people know that either. Only a few die-hards.

I quit New York State in December 1970 and went to Guam in January 1971 to become a wildlife biologist again, at a salary one-third less. I wanted to travel and photograph the world. I spent six years there and loved every minute of it, including the making of new enemies. I used Guam as a jumping-off spot to travel and photograph the world during my vacation periods. The miseries and beauties of some twenty-nine countries and six continents yielded to my cameras. I quit working

in 1977. Never regretted it either. I now live on a farm in Aurora, climb trees during the deer-hunting season, fish, and do some forest thinning, putting to use some of Professor Recknagel's instructions on how to thin a woodlot. And of course I still travel and photograph.

What did Connecticut Hill teach me? I can't really say that it taught me anything, but it may have strengthened my resolve to pursue the conservation field at Cornell. I marveled at the fact that I could do that for a living and get paid for it. I would never get rich at it, but it was satisfying in ways too numerous to mention. In retrospect, the Hill must have embedded the message that all environmental research, like all other research, is tedious and time-consuming and that there is usually a cause behind an effect. The trick was to find the cause and prove it to be so. It showed me that that process was no piece of cake. One had to work hard to complete a bit of research.

We Hillers amassed a tremendous amount of data, which most of us were not aware of contributing, as we made our small observations. I worked only two springs flushing grouse. The core workers who worked summers and all year deserve the credit for most of the findings. I admire the authors for putting it all together. The resulting book is still regarded as the ruffed grouse bible, a definitive game-research classic. All of us are proud to have been a part of it.

Looking back, I wish I could be a boy just entering Cornell again. This time I think I'd skip football.

The 1982 reunion. Standing: *Al Hall, John Schempp, Steve Fordham, Al Bromley, Bill Severinghaus, Nick Drahos, and Jim Otis.* Kneeling: *Art Hawkins, Joe Dell, Earl Westervelt, Dick Reynolds, Paul Christner, John Whalen, and Paul Kelsey.*

CHAPTER TWELVE

Echoes of the Hill

INFLUENCES ON LIVES AND CAREERS

FROM THE VERY START it was clear that the grouse investigation would spawn many outstanding careers in the wildlife field. Gardiner Bump left after the first year to direct the investigation statewide and then became superintendent of game. A year later Bob Darrow was tapped to organize the project's Adirondack study unit and then branched into studies of white-tailed deer in the same region.

Reflecting on the sixteen years from the start of the investigation to 1946, conservation commissioner Perry B. Duryea, in his foreword to the survey's printed report, termed this training function for young wildlife workers "probably one of the most valuable by-products" of the investigation. He continued:

Innumerable students at Cornell and a number of employees of the Department cut their teeth on one or more of the many phases of this study. In the ensuing years, many of these young men have grown up to take over positions of high responsibility in our own Department, in the Conservation Departments of other states and in the Federal conservation agencies.

Most Hillers commented on the long-term influences of the investigation they had experienced. One significant influence was a notable enrichment in their lives. Another influence was on the direction of their careers.

After college Paul Christner returned to Genesee County for a lifetime of farming, but what he gained from his Hill experience has stayed with him his whole life: "I shall always be thankful for having worked on the Hill. Although I grew up on a farm, it was the Hill experience that opened my eyes to the wonders of nature I would otherwise not have enjoyed. The good character of the fellow Hillers made the work a pleasure and has resulted in lasting friendships."

Another Hiller who commented on the sustained benefits of the contact with nature on the Hill was Warren Hewes:

While my work after college was not always closely related to my studies at Cornell, I have never for a moment regretted the time spent in those classrooms and on Connecticut Hill. Because of those studies and experiences, I have had much better insight and appreciation of everyday life, whether working in my garden, walking through woods and parks, taking outdoor pictures, or traveling in this country or abroad. It has improved my powers of detailed observation and understanding of the ecology of my surroundings throughout my lifetime.

Greenie Chase cites deep influences that have persisted: "I'm sure the Hill influenced my desire for employment—it set a standard of living and understanding of basic life for me and my wife. It made me aware of the fourth dimension, life perception within the natural law and its true meaning."

Ben Bradley's life was also enriched: "Many aspects of woods, trees, weather, and wildlife have all contributed to leaving deeply etched memories that make the experience a lifetime treasure."

Most of those whose careers were influenced by their days on the Hill started out with at least some knowledge of wildlife work and an interest in pursuing it. In fact, almost half of them were already focused on a career in wildlife. For them the Hiller experience furnished a direct link to their objective.

The circumstances Bob Darrow relates are an illustration:

I have had an interest in wildlife for as long as I can remember. Along with other boys in the village of Ashville (Chautauqua County), I hunted, fished, and trapped when the seasons were open. I was especially attracted to birds, and I went to Cornell with the purpose of studying ornithology (the local people who knew of that considered me a little loco). Consequently I was associated with Dr. A. A. Allen when he was helping recruit students as field observers at the outset of the ruffed grouse investigation on Connecticut Hill. My work there led to a permanent appointment in the Bureau of Game in the NYS Conservation Department and to work with other species, especially deer. It all culminated in my serving as editor of the *New York Fish and Game Journal* for nearly thirty-five years. Without the opportunity for participation in the project on the Hill, my career would undoubtedly have been very different.

Don Foley had also been committed to a wildlife career since an early age:

I don't think anyone could have swayed me from my course. When, in talking to someone in higher education in the NYS Education Department, I learned there was a conservation and wildlife program at Cornell (rather than the forester or ranger training at Syracuse), my fate was sealed.

◆ *The Hiller reunion in 1982 was deemed special, for it was the fifty-year celebration of the beginning of the Connecticut Hill Survey. It attracted at least twenty-five Hillers. Those pictured here are Mason Lawrence, Chuck Mason, Ralph Colson, Don Spittler, Harvey Warner (culturing a beard at the request of a daughter so he could be so embellished when he gave her away at her wedding), and Paul Kelsey.*

But getting to know the great teachers, going on field trips with them, and especially being given the responsibility of a section, a clipboard, and a couple of other people—with the idea that we were looking for facts that would give us some answers to great mysteries—those were the greatest spurs to putting me over the top. Everything before that was fine and interesting and alluring—but now I was focused!

I'm sure many of us truly learned to observe on the survey: tracks, scats, a faint trail, a feather or two, a shining eye. Maybe I'm jaundiced—do computer biologists have much of this ability?

For Art Hawkins the experience was "a link in the chain of events that shaped my career in wildlife management":

I didn't realize then how important the experience would prove. It provided the best on-the-job training in wildlife management available at the time. It opened doors that might have remained closed were it not for the entry on my résumé that I had participated in the first major grouse study. It provided contacts that proved useful at various stages of my career and continue to the present.

Remove this link from the chain of events, and who knows what might have happened? And so I say cheers to all who worked on the grouse survey! Long live the Hill in all its splendor! May its grouse continue to prosper!

Bill Severinghaus's grouse-survey experience qualified him for a temporary post during the second term of his junior year, and that post led to a career:

Near Christmas 1936 life ended for the man who was to have taken a deer-survey job in the Moose River Plains in January. I was without enough money for the second term at Cornell, so I told Frank Edminster and asked if I could do the deer-survey work. Ed got the job for me during January–March 1937, working under Bob Darrow.

My grouse-survey work led directly to my future big-game work, the work of my entire career.

The initial boost that Sarge Underhill experienced after he completed his Ph.D. in 1948 brought many opportunities within a few years:

My graduate major was fisheries, initially under George Embody and Charlie Mottley, but my wildlife minor with Art Allen and my work on the Hill really turned me toward game management. My first job was as a game research investigator with the NYS Conservation Department in charge of pheasant research. When I got out of the army, in 1946, I took a job as the regional game manager for the southern tier of New York State, with headquarters in Ithaca. I went from there to the Massachusetts Fish and Game Association in 1948, to become engaged in public relations and lobbying. It wasn't until I became director of New Jersey Fish and Game, in 1950, that fisheries became part of my responsibilities.

After the war Chuck Mason was able to pick up his career where he had left off:

Upon discharge from the army air corps, I returned to the Conservation Department and to wildlife research. Assignments included waterfowl and upland game birds. My most notable success was with the turkey-restoration program.

After many years as a field biologist, I transferred to the central office to work on fish and game budgets and, later, long-range planning.

Neal Kuhn found his niche in science teaching:

When I got out of the navy, I made several trips to Albany and talked with Gardiner Bump. He was pleased with my background in wildlife ecology, and I was offered a job with the Conservation Department as a biologist. I had to decide between teaching and the job with the Conservation Department. Teaching won out. I taught school in California and spent summers as a ranger naturalist with the national parks at Kings Canyon and Muir Woods.

Like other participants, Mason Lawrence feels that his experiences provided a practical foundation for his subsequent career:

My first work on Connecticut Hill was as a game technician in the summer after my sophomore year. I worked July and August for the Resettlement Administration under Bob Cameron marking trees to be cut to improve forest growth and wildlife habitat.

I took the game-management course in the ornithology department the second year it was taught, spring term 1937, I believe. The course was given by Dr. Allen and Eddie Edminster and assisted by Walt Crissey, who had taken the course the first year it was offered. There was a lab from

8:00 a.m. to 1:00 p.m. on Saturdays, and we spent most Saturdays on Connecticut Hill doing grouse-survey work on one or more sites.

Both of those activities—stand-improvement marking and the game-management course—gave me practical experience and knowledge in the game-management field, which were useful to me over the years in my work in conservation administration.

Don Schierbaum gives us the essence of the powerful opportunity afforded those who worked on the Hill: "Working on the grouse survey was a practical experience for a career in wildlife research and management. It provided us a chance to show our abilities and weeded out many who were not dedicated to a wildlife career."

For another group of Hillers whose career direction pointed less firmly toward wildlife, the survey experience reinforced and elevated their interests. George Elliott and Chuck Mason were so affected. Indeed both say that the Hill helped confirm their interests. George recalls: "My time on the Hill helped confirm my desire to find an outdoor job that I enjoyed doing. My time in the U.S. Army also convinced me that outdoors was where I was most happy. No desk job for this guy."

In a similar vein Chuck relates:

Although I already had substantial informal field experience, the grouse survey exposed me to the discipline of systematic data collection required for meaningful analysis. The Hill experience also introduced me to the office staff of Crissey, Bromley, Schierbaum, and Hall—people already employed in the emerging wildlife field. That experience, coupled with Lee Kutz's course in wildlife management, confirmed my interest in making this field my lifework.

But probably most importantly, the Hill experience gave the office staff a chance to evaluate each of us under a variety of conditions. Their recommendations were nearly essential for those of us who wanted to start our careers with New York.

For two other Hillers, Royce Brower and Harvey Warner, the same kinds of advantages led them to positions with federal agencies. Royce recounts:

Working on the Hill increased my interest in wildlife management and added experience in the field. It also gave me the opportunity to work on the grouse survey at the Adirondack unit. Those experiences, plus a longtime interest in wildlife, especially birds and mammals, helped give me the incentive to take the federal civil service exam for junior biologist. That led me directly into my career with the U.S. Soil Conservation Service.

Harvey evaluates his experience in these terms:

Wildlife conservation was a career objective before I entered college. The grouse survey offered the opportunity to gain that much-needed job experience. Working with others with similar interests,

and getting to meet people already in career jobs in wildlife research and management, reinforced my desire to pursue conservation work.

After discharge from the military, in 1946, I worked for the NYS Conservation Department for a number of years doing land-acquisition work throughout the state. Then I joined the U.S. Fish and Wildlife Service and continued in land-acquisition work in the thirteen states of the northeast region. Some of the things I learned on the grouse survey helped both in the military and in conservation work. Probably the most helpful were the feeling of being at home in the woods, a sharpened sense of observation, and an increased ability to keep oriented in unfamiliar surroundings.

To another Hiller, Ralph Colson, the Hill represented an eye-opening introduction to wildlife conservation:

Working on the Hill introduced me to the upcoming field of wildlife research and management. I entered Cornell because I was interested in birds, and I had heard about Arthur A. Allen, professor of ornithology. For two years after high school I worked at a job (large-building construction) that I didn't particularly like, so I decided to apply to the College of Agriculture, where tuition was free to New York State residents. I had no idea at the time where that might lead me, because no guidance counselors in high school had ever mentioned a field such as wildlife conservation. Working on the

spring grouse survey really opened my eyes to the possibilities of the field as a career with the NYS Conservation Department.

When he entered Cornell at seventeen, "city born and reared," Joe Dell didn't have any idea what he wanted to study. He only knew that he didn't want to farm for a living:

However, college requirements meant I had to take farm-practice training for two years. Then, near the end of my freshman year, I learned in discussions with friends (Schempp, Whalen, Westervelt, etc.) that the grouse survey was an alternative to farm practice. I applied for the survey, was accepted, and on my first day at work was hooked; the Hill opened up a totally new world. The concept of a career in wildlife quickly defined the curriculum I would follow for the next three years.

Over the ensuing years I have frequently reflected on my good fortune in starting college at a time when conservation and wildlife management were evolving rapidly, both in concept and as professional careers. Coupling that with the opportunity along the way to work and associate with fabulous people with intense dedication and talent tells me that fate has indeed been kind. I owe it all to my early luck in finding a way out of farm practice and from the revelation that came to me from exposure to the grouse survey and Connecticut

◆ *A gathering at Cornell's Arnot Forest during the Hiller reunion in June 1988, held to mark the Hillers' initial success in endowing a student summer internship. The authentic Alaskan totem pole (upper left) was used as a logo by the Civilian Conservation Corps camp located there. Left to right: Steve Fordham, Neal Kuhn, Bob Darrow, Mason Lawrence, Gary Goff, Bill Severinghaus, Jane Lawrence, Dan Decker, Harlan Brumsted, Brad Griffin (wearing sunglasses), Don Spittler (front), Don Schaufler (behind Brad), Ray Oglesby, Jim Otis, Paul Christner, Robert Demeree, Ruth Otis, Florence Hall, Ward Dukelow, Al Hall, Bruce Manuel, Lois Reynolds, Gil Ott, Dick Reynolds, Royce Brower, and Harvey Warner. Gary, Dan, Don Schaufler, and Ray were participating staff from Cornell's Department of Natural Resources; Robert, Ward, and Bruce were representatives from region 7 (Cortland) of the New York State Department of Environmental Conservation; and Gil was from Cornell's development office.*

Wayne Trimm's career, like Westy's, began in management and then came to concentrate in education. His is the perspective of an artist:

The Hill reinforced my love for fieldwork and my understanding of how vital it is for accurate information. I had been doing that sort of thing since I was eight, when I used to take a sketchbook to the field to record things I saw or experienced. I still do, having traveled over most of the world doing paintings, drawings, and photography of wildlife and its environment. When working on the *Conservationist* magazine, I spent as much time as possible afield to add to my references for writing and illustration. I was with the magazine for nearly forty years.

When I was a district wildlife manager out West, I used techniques learned on the Hill in my population surveys of resident game species.

Walt Crissey's career was repeatedly influenced by his experiences on Connecticut Hill:

After the war I returned to the Conservation Department and was stationed in Albany. The department decided to invest in a war-surplus observation plane (a Stinson L-5) and use it to develop more-efficient methods for collecting wildlife research and management information. As an experienced pilot, and in addition to other duties, I was assigned to develop the techniques.

The field of effort included deer, fox-pheasant relationships, muskrat and beaver distribution and abundance, illegal fish netting, hunting and fishing pressures, and waterfowl surveys.

The successful development of techniques for measuring the size and distribution of waterfowl in New York led to my being offered a position with U.S. Fish and Wildlife, which I accepted in July 1949. In the years that followed, the insight I had gained regarding sampling techniques, representativeness of data, and statistical procedures while working with grouse-survey data had a marked influence on the gradual development of other surveys. The other surveys, measuring waterfowl numbers and distribution, survival determinations, and harvest by hunters, are still operating in North America today.

Don Spittler's career in state and federal government included both resource management and land appraisal and acquisition, areas that present challenging human dimensions. He is also a highly trained military leader with long experience, both in World War II active duty and in the army reserves during peacetime. Don reflects and comments on what it means to have been a Hiller:

Many Hillers who aspired to a career in wildlife were motivated by a passion for nature. To embark on a career in wildlife management on that foundation, with only an academic education, left much to the element of chance. The opportunity to work on the Hill concurrently with academic studies disclosed the unknown—a revelation! The experience opened the doors to the application of academic education for the practical solution of management problems and opened the vista to a career in wildlife management.

Workdays became seminars, wherein the exchange of knowledge and opinions broadened one's perspective and sharpened the tools of observation. The diversity of work habits and attitudes among the workers exposed the human element, which was to become a future challenge in personnel management. Determination to persevere under strain and duress, concentration on the mission, sympathy and understanding for fellow workers, dedication to a work ethic, and a deep appreciation for the complexities of nature are everlasting traits attributable to experiences on Connecticut Hill.

Collectively, these traits formed habitual attitudes that enhanced the quality of the career performance of the Hillers and expanded the dimensions of their personal lives.

Index